★ ★ ★ ★ ★

FEDERAL CAREERS IN
LAW ENFORCEMENT

★ ★ ★ ★ ★

FEDERAL CAREERS IN
LAW ENFORCEMENT

Russ Smith, Ph.D.

IMPACT PUBLICATIONS
Manassas Park, VA

Library of Congress Cataloguing-in-Publication Data

Smith, Russ
    Federal careers in law enforcement / Russ Smith.
        p.   cm.
    1-57023-035-8 (paper)
        1. Law enforcement—Vocational guidance—United States.
    2. Police—Vocational guidance—United States. 3. Civil service
    positions—United States. 4. United States—Officials and
    employees—Selection and appointment. I. Title.
    HV8143.S63 1996
        363.2′023′73—dc20   95-51113
                                                                CIP

For information on distribution or quantity discount rates, Tel. 703/361-7300, FAX 703/335-9486, e-mail: impactp@impactpublications.com, or write to: Sales Department, IMPACT PUBLICATIONS, 9104-N Manasas Drive, Manassas Park, VA 22111-5211. Distributed to the trade by National Book Network, 4720 Boston Way, Suite A, Lanham, MD 20706. Tel. 301/459-8696.

CONTENTS

Chapter 5

Starting a Career in Law Enforcement **47**

Chapter 6

**The Application Action Plan
and Career Resources** **58**

Appendices **73**

ACKNOWLEDGMENTS

Ron and Caryl Krannich were instrumental in bringing this book to print, for which help I cannot thank them enough. Legions of personnel officers were also very helpful in collecting information for this book and series.

The opinions expressed here are those of the author. They are not necessarily shared by Impact Publications, the U.S. Army, the Office of Personnel Management, or anyone else with a god-like power over the author.

★ ★ ★ ★ ★

FEDERAL CAREERS IN
LAW ENFORCEMENT

Chapter 1

1 OO,OOO LAW
ENFORCEMENT JOBS

I f you believe most public law enforcement jobs are found at the state and local levels, think again. The federal government is the single largest employer of law enforcement personnel. Indeed, it employs over 100,000 law enforcement officials. Found in numerous agencies, these law enforcement jobs are interesting, relatively secure, pay well, and lead to career advancement. Given recent cutbacks in government employment, federal law enforcement jobs appear to be some of the best jobs available. They should continue so in the foreseeable future.

The people of the United States have long relied upon the services of a few highly-trained professionals to enforce national laws and the provisions of the Constitution. Whether we speak of the F.B.I. pursuing America's "Ten Most Wanted," agents of the U.S. Customs Service enforcing import laws, or Wildlife Service agents hunting poachers on federal lands, we are speaking of federal law enforcement careers[1].

Jobs and Applications

Throughout this book we identify ways to begin a federal career in law enforcement. While some books examine different types of federal law enforcement jobs and describe agencies, most provide little information on how to go about applying for and landing the job. In other words, they leave out the critical details necessary for landing the job—vacancy announcements, applications packages, and personnel procedures. That's our task in this book: outline the application process and show how to make it work in your favor.

Anyone who wants to pursue such a career will normally begin in an 'entry level' job. Depending on the federal organization, this entry level job may be a GS-1811-05 Criminal Investigator or a GS-905-11 Attorney.[2] To get one

---

[1]The Federal Bureau of Investigation, a bureau or sub-unit in the U.S. Department of Justice, has for many years published a list of people who are accused of breaking federal law(s) and the most eagerly-sought are called the "Most Wanted." The Customs Service is one of the law enforcement divisions of the U.S. Department of the Treasury. The U.S. Fish and Wildlife Service in the U.S. Department of the Interior has a network of wildlife law enforcement agents.

[2]Most federal jobs are identified by a classification number. The first part, GS or GM or WG, for example, indicate that the job is General Schedule, GS Manager, or Wage Grade. The next numbers identify the job series—905 is the number for attorneys. The last number is the starting pay grade. These terms will be explained in more detail later in the book.

of these jobs, you need to respond to a specific job announcement. Generally, applications sent to an agency are
ignored unless they are in response to an announced
opening. (The exception is when an agency sets up an
Applicant Supply File or **register**). Once you've found an
announcement, a successful application requires the
careful construction of an application packet which clearly
indicates that the applicant has the right background and
education to apply for the job.

Throughout this century, the process of applying for a
federal (as well as a state or local) government job has
been evolving toward a way to select the most qualified
person.[3] Various ways were tried to help managers find the
most qualified employees. One trend was to rely on
"objective" or unbiased comparisons of applicants' skills
with what a job required; people who met or exceeded
requirements would be eligible for hiring. In addition to
standard application forms, such as the SF-171 (Standard
Form 171) or the OF-612, resumes which follow the federal
format are also accepted, in most cases, as the core of an
application packet. Anyone applying for a law enforcement
position must also be prepared to provide other information, and should expect a series of tests before being
approved for selection.

The Book

The purpose of this book is to inform people about entry
level federal jobs in law enforcement. We will also show
you how to find out about job vacancies (announcements),

---

[3] A good review of these changes is in "Selection of
Personnel" by Robert H. Elliott, in *Handbook on Public
Personnel Administration and Labor Relations*, Jack Rabin
et al.(eds.), New York: Marcel Dekkar, Inc, 1983, 123-57.

how to identify the kinds of jobs available, the agencies which normally recruit for these jobs, and we will give some guidance on how to create a successful job application packet.[4]

We begin in **Chapter 2** by examining the major jobs in law enforcement as well as identifying the key agencies having law enforcement officials.

Chapter 3 looks at myths and misperceptions some people have about the process of applying for a federal job and working in law enforcement for the federal government. A short quiz tests you on both of these topics. The balance of the chapter debunks some of the common myths about each topic.

Chapter 4 provides background to the federal government's hiring methods. We provide a thumbnail sketch of the federal government and how people are hired by federal organizations. A subtle, but major factor in the federal hiring process is that the focus is not on hiring people (be they the "most skilled," "disadvantaged," veteran, or whatever) but rather **the focus is on filling positions**. As many former military personnel know, battles cannot be won unless you know your "enemy." Not everyone who applies for a federal job is "at war" with the federal government, of course, but this analogy does help prepare you for the form while **Chapter 5** describes the position management process.

Chapter 5 describes the variety of federal jobs in law enforcement. We begin by identifying where the jobs are, then look at the qualifications required of applicants for the jobs. We also identify some of the many programs used by agencies to recruit women and minorities into these entry

---

[4]More thorough help in applying for a federal job can be found in *Federal Applications That Get Results*, by Russ Smith, Ph.D., Manassas Park, VA: Impact Publications, 1996.

level jobs. Finally, we review what one might expect at the start of his or her federal career in law enforcement.

In Lewis Carrol's story **Alice in Wonderland**, at one point, she is walking through a forest and comes to a fork in the trail and sees Cheshire Cat sitting on a branch..

> *"Would you tell me, please, which way I ought to go from here?"*
> *"That depends a good deal on where you want to get to," said the Cat.*
> *"I don't much care where," said Alice.*
> *"Then it doesn't matter which way you go," said the Cat.*
> *"So long as I get somewhere," Alice added as an explanation.*

Unless you know how your application will be evaluated, what kinds of information will be used by personnel specialists to rate your application, it is hard to know what to put in your application and what to leave out. How can you prepare your most effective replies? The main problems with many applications is that people either ramble on for several paragraphs without providing enough information to evaluate their qualifications or use jargon that is misunderstood or not credited. What about your background is relevant for the job you seek? How do you ensure that what you write will be understood by people who read and evaluate your application? Regardless of the form you use, you need a way to effectively show that you have the education, work experience, or knowledge, skills and abilities sought by the hiring agency.

The last chapter, **Chapter 6**, describes the most important steps to follow in applying for a federal job in law enforcement. The first objective is to find a job opening. Where do you go to find a job announcement? How do you translate it into English? The second objective is to discuss

the typical qualifications expected of applicants. These
standards are the minimum requirements one must reach
to get a job in law enforcement with the federal government. Special programs in place to help recruit women
and minorities apply for jobs are also described here.
Finally, we give some idea of what one can expect in the
first year or so after being hired into a law enforcement
position.

This final chapter provides an "action plan" to guide you
through the federal job application process. Here you'll
find a step-by-step plan and check list to help you track
your applications. The action plan will be your guide to
implementing the ideas described here for writing a strong
federal job application.[5]

Upon completion of this material, you should have an
understanding of how to start a career in law enforcement
with the federal government. Of course, no **guarantees** are
given here; we cannot anticipate all problems that may
arise with one person's application for a job. However, the
advice contained here on applying for a federal job comes
from people currently working for the federal government,
including some of its personnel specialists. If an agency
follows normal federal practices in filling a position, then
the advice here should prepare you to sell yourself in the
most positive way for a law enforcement position.

The **appendices** provide a number of resources to assist
you in pursuing your career. The serious job applicant will
have to contact several government agencies or private
firms to acquire job announcements, supplemental materials and forms, and a copy of *X-118 Qualification Standards*. The first appendix has a list of the terms used in the
federal hiring process. Later appendices include descrip-

---

[5]For more detailed help in preparing an application, see
Federal Applications that Get Results, Russ Smith, Ph.D.,
Manassas Park, VA: Impact Publications, 1996.

tions of federal pay rates, where to go for information and announcements, several standard forms you may need, and examples of job announcements. Finally, there is a copy of the action plan, in a checklist format, for doing a job search and an application form. The action plan identifies each step to be pursued in the process of completing an application packet for a particular job announcement.

Good luck in starting your career in law enforcement. If you follow our advice on how to apply for a federal job, your application should stand out from the crowd. You'll be putting your best foot forward for what may well be a most rewarding and exciting career in federal law enforcement.

Chapter 2

JOBS IN LAW ENFORCEMENT

The quote from *Alice in Wonderland* in the first chapter illustrates the idea that effective decisions or actions require a goal or plan. *If you don't know where you're going, it doesn't matter which path you take.* The purpose of this book is to identify how to find and successfully apply for federal jobs in law enforcement. Before getting into the details, the balance of this chapter describes the general characteristics of those jobs: what are the typical law enforcement jobs, where are they, and what are the basic qualifications for the jobs.

The Jobs

There were over *100,000* federal law enforcement jobs in 1993. A list of the more common types of law enforcement jobs, describing in general terms the kinds of work required, follows.[1] The GS-XXX phrase refers to the *job series* identifier; this is the common identifier for any federal job. The number in parentheses after the job series identifier is the number of positions of that type in the U.S. government in as of September 30, 1993[2]

- **Park Ranger, GS-025 (7,145).** Park rangers are responsible for enforcing laws, regulations and policies on federal park property. In addition to normal police duties of traffic control, investigation of crimes, preparing evidence for trials, and so forth, park rangers also are responsible for ensuring that visitors to parks are safe and that the parks, themselves, are protected from harm by visitors.

- **Security Specialist, GS-080 (6,695).** This position is responsible for personnel, physical, information, and industrial security in many agencies, and involves safeguarding information, personnel, and property from theft, loss, misuses, espionage or sabotage. Security specialists develop, evaluate, and implement security programs, policies or directions.

---

[1]The information here is summarized from federal *Position Classification Standard Handbooks* or *Position Qualification Standard Handbooks*. All are published by the U.S. Office of Personnel Management.

[2]"Full-Time Federal Civilian Employment in White- and Blue-Collar Occupations as of September 30, 1993," by Christine E. Steele, an Occupational Survey summary available from the Office of Personnel Management.

- **United States Marshal, GS-082 (489).** Marshals are involved in a range of law enforcement responsibilities, including serving writs and warrants issued by federal courts, tracing and arresting persons wanted under court warrants, seizing and disposing of property under court orders, handling prisoners, securing court facilities and staff, guarding witnesses and jurors, and other jobs directed by the Department of Justice.

- **Police Officers, GS-083 (8,845).** Police officers perform or supervise law enforcement work such as: prevention, detection and investigation of crimes, arrest or apprehension of suspects; and assisting civilians in emergencies.

- **Security Guard, GS-085 (5,463).** Security guards perform or supervise protective services work on federally owned or leased property, protect government equipment or property, and control access to federal property.

- **General Attorney, GS-905 (24,699).** Many attorneys are involved with the enforcement of federal laws and regulations. Their work can include investigations to obtain evidentiary data, or assisting people preparing for trials. Areas of work are in civil rights, customs, finance, immigration, or general law work, to name but a few.

- **General Inspection, Investigation and Compliance Officer, GS-1801/1802 (5,771/4,517).** These are 'catch-all' positions for people who supervise or perform inspection work, investigations, or other tasks concerning enforcement of federal laws, regulations or other guidelines. GS-1801/1802 is used when another position does not cover the work done. Unique or one-of-a-kind law enforcement positions may be represented by GS-1801/1802, such as the Game Warden position described in Chapter 4.

- **General Investigator, GS-1810 (4,796).** General investigators supervise or perform investigations of people or organizations involved with the federal government. General investigators perform, for example, background checks, security investigations, and other studies.

- **Criminal Investigator, GS-1811 (32,638).** Criminal investigators supervise or perform investigations relating to alleged or suspected violations of criminal laws. This includes maintaining surveillance, performing undercover work, investigating crimes, and other work in support of U.S. attorneys.

- **Immigration Inspector, GS-1816 (4,497).** Immigration inspectors enforce laws affecting immigrants and alien residents of the U.S. This includes administering laws, regulations and policies concerning entry to the country, as well as detaining or apprehending violators.

- **Customs Inspector, GS-1890 (6,470).** Customs inspectors enforce and administer laws concerning the import or export of merchandise. They are involved in a variety of duties involved with the control of imports and exports including inspecting goods, preventing smuggling and fraud, and assuring collection of import duties.

- **Border Patrol Agent, GS-1896 (3,965).** Border patrol agents are involved in law enforcement work preventing smuggling or illegal entry of aliens into the U.S., apprehending people who violate laws concerning the entry of goods and people into the country.

Where Are The Jobs?

Appendix D has a list of federal agencies which have law enforcement jobs. This section will briefly review some of the major players in the federal government; those activities which typically have openings in law enforcement jobs. The best sources for job announcements are Federal Employment Information Centers (see Appendix C), *Federal Career Opportunities* or *Federal Digest* (see Chapter 5), or agency personnel offices (see Appendix D).

- **Inspectors General.** Every federal department, such as Agriculture, Commerce, State, Treasury, Housing and Urban Development, has law enforcement jobs in their Inspector General offices. As will be shown in Chapter 4, an Inspector General office typically has a number of GS-1810 and 1811 inspector positions. The mission of an Inspector General office is to investigate the department's employees, as well as the department's suppliers, contractors, and clients/customers. Employees are investigated for fraud, waste, or abuse of government property or authority. Suppliers, contractors and clients/customers are also investigated for providing supplies or services below standards requested by the agency, attempts to defraud the organization (either by falsifying records or outright misrepresentation), and other types of crimes.

- **Forest Service, Department of Agriculture.** The Forest Service uses Park Rangers and other law enforcement jobs (such as criminal investigators) to protect the nation's forests and woodlands and detect crimes (such as hunting violations, stealing resources, vandalism, and even suppressing illegal drug activities).

- **Department of Defense.** Most of the white collar law enforcement jobs are in the Department of Defense. Also, most military posts in this country employ one or more Game Wardens (GS-1801/1802) to supervise 'natural' areas of the post (a large army base, such as Fort Hood, Texas, for example, often has hundreds of acres of land protected by wardens who, like Park Rangers, are involved in detecting crimes and protecting the areas from misuse). White collar jobs in Defense activities include police officers, security guards, general and criminal investigators, and attorneys. The Department, as well as each Service within the Department (Army, Navy, Air Force) has a large Inspector General activity, with offices around the world. Other employers in Defense include the Defense Investigative Service, Air Force Office of Special Investigations, Army Criminal Investigation Command, and the Naval Criminal Investigative Service. All conduct investigations of alleged criminal acts in procurement or contract related fraud, corruption, abuse of authority, and theft of federal property.

- **Department of the Interior.** Most of the nation's Park Rangers work for the Department of the Interior's National Park Service. The Department also extensively uses general and criminal investigators in the Bureau of Land Management and the U.S. Fish and Wildlife Service. While mostly concerned with the safety and security of national parks and recreation areas, increasingly, law enforcement officials of the Interior Department are also involved in curtailing illegal drug activity in national parks and, in a few cases, curtailing illegal immigration and smuggling.

- **Department of Justice.** The Bureau of Prisons employed, in 1993, over 11,000 Correctional Institution Administrators/Correctional Officers (GS-006/GS-007), to supervise or control prisoners in the federal prison system. A large number of investigator and attorney positions are also used by the Drug Enforcement Administration, the Federal Bureau of Investigation, and the Immigration and Naturalization Service. The latter is also the primary employer for immigration inspectors (GS-1816). Finally, the U.S. Marshals Service has about 500 U.S. Marshals (GS-082) to enforce federal laws and federal court decisions.

- **Department of State.** As will be shown in Chapter 4, the Department of State employs, among others, security specialists and general inspectors to identify and eliminate security hazards for diplomatic personnel and facilities.

- **Department of the Treasury.** The Bureau of Alcohol, Tobacco and Firearms uses general and criminal investigator positions as Special Agents to enforce federal laws and regulate industries pertaining to alcohol, tobacco, firearms and explosives, curtail illegal traffic in firearms and explosives, and collect federal tax revenues on alcohol and tobacco. The

Internal Revenue Service uses investigator positions to pursue violators of federal tax codes. The IRS' Internal Security Division investigates alleged criminal acts by IRS employees (taking bribes, embezzling, or disclosing tax records), conducts background investigations of potential employees, and special investigations at the request of the Secretary. The Customs Service inspectors work at over 300 ports of entry to the U.S., assessing and collecting customs duties, taxes, and fees, controlling access of goods and people to the U.S., preventing fraud and smuggling, and helping suppress smuggling of illegal drugs and pornography.

These are but a few of the organizations in the federal government which have law enforcement jobs. More information about the federal government organizations in the next chapter, plus a list of similar federal organizations (with law enforcement jobs) in Appendix D, will round out a description of where the jobs are.

Qualifications

Obviously, law enforcement jobs with the federal government vary considerably, from security guards to attorneys. So too do the qualifications for jobs vary. While some generalizations can be made here, the best source of information is an actual job announcement, identifying the education and experience required of applicants.

Educational Experience. Many of the jobs here may require a college degree at grades seven or higher.[3] Even the lower grades may require some college hours, such as an Associate Arts degree in fields such as criminal justice, political science, sociology, or related disciplines. Grades nine or higher typically require a baccalaureate degree and even a master's degree or post-graduate class work. Fortunately, work experience can compensate for educational deficiencies.

Work Experience. Two types of work experience are important: general and specialized. General experience includes such things as working with others, ability to communicate, ability to supervise others, and ability to work independently of supervisors. Specialized experience here refers to experience related to the job, such as knowledge of federal laws, ability to work with firearms, ability to conduct surveillance operations, and so forth. The good thing is that for grades 5 through 9, specialized experience can often compensate for insufficient education. For example, if working with firearms is important to a job and an applicant has considerable experience here, that may eliminate the need for a bachelor's degree in criminal justice. The key word is that each job series and announcement has different requirements; you need to examine the announcements and get a feel for the education and experience requirements for a GS-1811-9 (grade 9 criminal investigator). Some of this is explained more fully in the next two chapters.

---

[3]As will be shown in the next chapter, federal jobs have *grades*, from 1 through 15, with 15 the highest grade. Entry-level jobs *normally* begin around grade 4 or 5, but this varies from series to series. Attorney jobs often begin at grade 9, for example.

The bottom line for this chapter is that there are a large number of law enforcement jobs with the federal government, over 100,000 in 1993 alone. The jobs range from game wardens and park rangers tracking poachers through investigators hunting fraud, waste and abuse of government authority, to attorneys preparing cases for trial. Given the variety of jobs and organizations involved, the next chapter tries to show how the federal government is organized, and how positions are filled. The way the system operates will be crucial for anyone applying for a federal job. If you don't know the rules used to screen applications, your application stands a good chance of being rejected.

Chapter 3

MYTHS AND REALITIES

Test Your Job Application Smarts

The following section tests your knowledge of federal careers in law enforcement, the federal application process and how to get a federal job. A series of statements are presented. Circle one of the five numbers following each question to indicate whether you: 1) Strongly Agree; 2) Agree; 3) Have no opinion; 4) Disagree or 5) Strongly Disagree with the statement.

1. You need a college degree to qualify for most federal jobs.

    1   2   3   4   5

2. Federal jobs in law enforcement are like police chasing robbers.

    1   2   3   4   5

3. A professional-quality *resume* can be used to apply for any federal job.

      1   2   3   4   5

4. Law enforcement jobs are just in the FBI, the Secret Service or the DEA.

      1   2   3   4   5

5. Anyone can complete a job application, no special knowledge is required.

      1   2   3   4   5

6. An exam has to be taken to get any federal jobs.

      1   2   3   4   5

7. There are no law enforcement jobs which require a college degree.

      1   2   3   4   5

8. A background in the military will not help someone get a federal job in law enforcement.

      1   2   3   4   5

Now go back through the list and add the number circled with each statement. If the total score is less than 32 then some of your knowledge of the federal government or the job application process is based on commonly-held misconceptions or myths. The next section briefly addresses each of these myths; later chapters will deal with each in more detail.

Federal Jobs Myths and Realities

MYTHS	REALITIES
1: You have to have a college degree, or at least some college credits, before "they" will even look at your job application.	Depends on the job. An attorney or auditor probably should have cracked a college book or two sometime during his or her life. However, the federal government recognizes alternatives to college education, including the General Education Development (GED) equivalency certificate, technical and vocational schools, and in some cases, just work experience. That is, many of the positions will allow you to substitute relevant work experience for college education. The trick is to know what education or experience is relevant to the job you want.
2: I don't want to work in an office pushing paper, so I'll never apply for a federal job in law enforcement.	Federal jobs in law enforcement vary from agency to agency. Jobs such as attorneys with the Securities and Exchange Commission, or Auditors with the Inspector General's office in the Department of Health and Human Services are usually 'office jobs.' Many aspects of the work of FBI Special Agents can also involve work in an office. However, jobs such as Forest Service National Park Service rangers, U.S. Customs Service agents

can require applicants to spend time in the great outdoors enforcing the law. Also, some organizations, especially the Bureau of Diplomatic Security in the State Department can require travel throughout the world protecting American government officials.

3: I'm trying to become a corrections officer with the Bureau of Prisons; I don't need to learn about the federal job application process.

You do if it is a federal job, chief! All federal jobs, both white collar and blue collar, require basically the same information from applicants for the job. This book can give you some insights in preparing an effective federal job application packet.

4: You need to pay a professional to make a good application package.

If you go to a professional resume service, they will ask you for the same information to put into an application package as you would need if you did it yourself. Of course, they SHOULD at least know what questions to ask you. Note that you will probably only get one version of your application packet (good for just one job vacancy application); if you want to apply to several jobs, most professional agencies will ask you to pay for each version of your application packet. Some of harder parts of preparing an application can be resolved with the information in this book.

5: Anyone can fill in the application for a federal job; there's no special trick involved.

Yes, of course, dealing with the federal government is very easy, simple, and uncomplicated. Sarcasm aside, there actually is a trick to the federal job application process. Your information will be evaluated by personnel specialists who will determine if you have the minimum qualifications for the job you are seeking. The determination will be made on the basis of what you put into your application packet. Now, these are **personnel** specialists, not specialists in law enforcement. They won't necessarily know the ins and outs of tax examiner work. What they will do is compare what you write with government- or agency-wide standards; if what you write CLEARLY indicates you meet the standards, then your application won't end up in the REJECTED file. So the trick is to explain yourself in terms the personnel specialists can understand. Make their work easier!

6: Federal jobs in law enforcement are basically like cops chasing robbers.

Well, yes, of course this is true on one level. By definition, federal law enforcement jobs involve 'cops' chasing 'robbers.'

However, this can include Forest Service Rangers chasing poachers on federal lands, Customs Service Agents chasing smugglers, or even auditors with an Inspector General office investigating their own agency for fraud, waste or mismanagement. FBI Forensic Specialists can hunt criminals by analyzing clues taken from crime scenes.

7: I don't want to take any exams to get a federal job.

Actually, very few federal jobs require exams. Above grade nine, most if not all federal jobs require relevant work experience (and maybe some college courses or degrees) instead of exams. There are many different kinds of law enforcement jobs with the federal government; depending on the job series and the requirements to do the work, you may not have to take an exam.

8: I don't have a college degree in criminology; there won't be a federal job given my background.

There are more different kinds of work with the federal government than most people imagine. For some federal jobs, the education requirements are often expressed as having a certain number of college semester hours (or equivalent) in RELATED disciplines. For example, the Criminal Investigator job series (GS-1811) as a Treasury Enforcement Agent requires twenty-four college semester hours in courses such as law enforcement, psychology, public affairs, business admin-stration, computer science, history, urban studies or lan-guage (the list goes on). A number of these courses are normally taken just meeting the general education require-ments at most colleges and universities; a few more classes could qualify some people for a job in this series as a Treasury Enforcement Agent. Alternatively, there are a number of other law enforce-ment job series that seek peo-ple with just a "liberal arts" background, as well as backgrounds in medicine, bio-logical sciences, or, yes, even crimi-nology! After some dig-ging, you can probably find a federal law enforcement job for almost any college major.

9: Federal jobs in law en-forcement are just in the FBI, the Secret Service or the DEA.

When you include investigator, accountant and auditor jobs in Inspector General offices, you can say that virtually every fed-eral organization has law en-forcement jobs. As will be shown in this book, there are many different types of careers in law enforcement available in the federal government.

10: I retire from the military soon; I'd like a federal job but I don't think my military experiences will be of any use in getting me a job.

People who have served in the military may actually have one of the best backgrounds for federal jobs. Almost every Military Occupational Specialty (MOS) has a federal civilian job series counterpart and many military skills can translate to civilian jobs in law enforcement. Recent alumni of the U.S. military should request DD Form 2586, "Verification of Military Experience and Training" from their transition office. This form itemizes the skills and training the vet received during his or her military service. The trick is to examine both the general qualification standards for a particular position, as well as the agency-specific standards and required knowledges, skills and abilities. Finally, when applications are evaluated, veterans, especially disabled veterans, receive preferential treatment, not only when applying for work, but during those dreaded Reduction-in-Force (RIF) exercises (when an agency is eliminating positions).

Chapter 4

WORKING FOR THE
FEDERAL GOVERNMENT

The process of applying for a federal job is currently undergoing its greatest change in almost thirty years. The precise role of various federal organizations in the hiring processes is undergoing change. For most of the last generation, Standard Form 171 (SF 171) has been the core of all application packets submitted by job seekers. Now, and probably for the next year or more, federal form OF 612 and federal style resumes are sometimes required as the core of job application packets. Electronic filing options are under study at the Office of Personnel Management and at selected agencies, such as the Department of Energy. This chapter reviews the increasingly more complex federal employment scene and the role of the application packet in that scene. The next chapter will use information presented here to focus on applying for federal careers in law enforcement.

General Schedule Jobs

Federal General Schedule (or GS)[1] jobs comprise over eighty percent of the federal work force. Most of the discussion here applies to GS jobs. Jobs in the GS are further grouped into twenty-one occupational groups (see Figure 3.1). Within each group (such as GS-1800) there are five or more **job series**, such as GS-1810 (General Investigators), GS-1812 (Game Law Enforcement Agents), GS-1811 (Criminal Investigators), and GS-1896 (Border Patrol Agents). Also, there are 'catch-all' job series 'GS-X01,' such as GS-301 or GS-1801, which are used when a position does not fit neatly into an existing job series but does fit into an occupational group. Appendix E has a complete listing of General Schedule occupational groups and job series.

As one might expect, the more difficult the work or responsibility of a position, the higher the pay grade (hereafter, just grade will be used). The federal government has attempted to be competitive in pay with other employers but is generally behind in some occupations. Federal employees in some "high cost of living" metropolitan areas, for example, now receive supplemental or "locality adjustment" pay. Hard to fill positions (such as secretarial positions) have, in the past, also received income supplements as inducements to remain in their positions. The Federal Pay Comparability Act, signed by President Bush in 1990, is supposed to raise federal white

---

[1]There are three major occupational groups of federal positions: the General Schedule, the Wage Grade (usually, trade, craft and labor positions), and the Excepted Service (such as political appointments).

collar salaries (shown in Appendix B) to levels competitive with the private sector. Beginning in January, 1994, pay increases for the 1.5 million federal white collar employees in General Schedule jobs are supposed to be based on wages for comparable private sector jobs **in their localities**! However, recent raises provided by Congress and approved by the President have fallen short of the levels mandated by the Comparability Act. Theoretically, by 2004 (assuming Congress and the President support the Act's provisions), the salaries of employees in General Schedule grades 1 through 15 should be comparable to those of private sector employees, judged on a case by case basis in twenty-six metropolitan areas with large concentrations of federal employees.[2]

The GS consists of eighteen grades for white collar workers. Further, grades one through fifteen are divided into ten steps (based on time-in-grade); grade sixteen has nine steps, seventeen has five steps, and eighteen has but one step. Usually, one can anticipate moving up a step every fifty-two weeks (for steps one through three), one hundred and four weeks (steps four through six), or one hundred and fifty-six weeks (steps seven through nine). Reaching step ten in a pay grade is the last step for that grade; a person would have to move to a new position (with a higher pay grade) to advance beyond step ten for a grade. Exceptional workers may also be given "quality step increases."

Appendix B shows the proposed 1995 GS pay plan for grades one through fifteen. Appendix B also shows pay schedules for other special "white collar" occupations, including the Foreign Service and law enforcement positions in the Metropolitan Washington, D.C. area.

---

[2]Some employees, such as some secretaries, will not receive this locality pay; other supplements may already apply.

·Figure 4.1
Federal Occupational Groups

Group No.	Group Title	Group No.	Group Title
GS-000	Miscellaneous	GS-1100	Business and Industry
GS-100	Social Science, Psychology and Welfare	GS-1200	Copyright, Patent and Trademark
GS-200	Personnel Management and Industrial Relations	GS-1300	Physical Sciences
		GS-1400	Library and Archives
GS-300	Administrative, Clerical and Office Services	GS-1500	Mathematics and Statistics
		GS-1600	Equipment, Facilities and Service
GS-400	Biological Sciences		
GS-500	Accounting and Budget	GS-1700	Education
GS-600	Medical, Hospital, Dental and Public Health	GS-1800	Investigation
		GS-1900	Quality Assurance, Inspection and Grading
GS-700	Veterinary Medical Science		
GS-800	Engineering and Architecture	GS-2000	Supply
GS-900	Legal and Kindred	GS-2100	Transportation
GS-1000	Public Information and Arts		

Position Management

The federal government, in an effort to treat employees and job applicants impartially, or at least without the pattern or practice of discrimination, manages positions, not people. That is, in a typical office, for example, a number of **positions** will be authorized or created and tasked to do the work of the office. Personnel specialists, working with the agency, will first identify, for the new position(s):

- What supervision will the position(s) receive;
- What supervision will the position(s) exercise; and
- What tasks will the position(s) perform.

After identifying what the position(s) will do, personnel specialists will then determine which occupational groups are required to do the work, and will determine the appropriate pay grade for that work, based on federal standards. People will then be recruited and hired based on the extent to which they match, in educational background and work experience, the knowledges, skills and other abilities required by the position.

Personnel specialists usually do not know enough about biochemistry, for example, to assign different biochemistry knowledges and skills to different federal grade levels. Specialists in biochemistry and other career groups provide personnel specialists the criteria for evaluating candidates for biochemistry positions. These are assembled into **position classification** or **qualification standards**, essentially lists of what tasks must be done at each grade in a job series.

The criteria used to evaluate candidates for government-wide careers have been standardized and serve as objective yardsticks for measuring a job applicant's background. Some government agencies go one step further, refining and clarifying the standards they wish to use in addition to the government-wide standards. When a person's application packet is evaluated by personnel specialists, then, the evaluation is made with reference to OPM (and, if any exist, agency) qualification standards. Job series in Appendix E which have an "*" are ones for which federal agencies have published agency-specific standards.

The way job applicants are evaluated is of considerable importance to someone applying for a federal job. Basically job applications must show how much education and work experience one has had in preparation for the vacant position. If **general** or **specialized experience** (discussed later in this chapter) at "the next lower grade" is required, an applicant has to show much time was spent doing the tasks of that lower grade, and must have enough time doing the tasks to meet the requirements.

For example, if an agency's standard is expressed as "at least one year's experience working with *LOTUS 1-2-3*, *Microsoft Excel*, or *Borland Quattro Pro*" (those are popular spreadsheet software trade names), then even though an applicant says she has five years experience with spread-sheet software, to a personnel specialist unfamiliar with computer jargon, the applicant lacks the appropriate experience. Even though the hiring official at the agency level does understand that *Excel* is a spreadsheet software program, the applicant's packet might not get sent to the hiring official simply because the information provided did not match what is in the standards and thus did not justify rating the applicant as qualified for the position!

In terms of education, an announcement for a grade eleven position might include as a standard a specific number of college hours in social science, history or English. Any applicants without those college hours do not meet that particular standard. Most job application packets include an official transcript to identify how much education was completed and to help the personnel specialist determine if enough credit hours in the right subjects have been earned.

Obviously, some effort has to be taken to successfully prepare an application packet. The applicant knows the facts of his or her work history, but how those facts are explained makes all the difference in preparing the right application packet. The SF 171 (or OF 612 or resume) is one (admittedly a major) part of an application package which will be reviewed (and possibly rejected), not on the quality of the typing done to prepare the package or how rich and exciting one's life has been, but **how well does the information provided correspond to position qualification standards!**[3]

---

[3]Insights on preparing a strong federal job application can be found in *Federal Applications that Get Results*, by Russ Smith, Ph.D., Impact Publications, Manassas Park, VA: 1996.

Example of Position Management

Figure 4.2 shows the positions in a hypothetical finance office. This hypothetical office has eleven positions or "slots" which can be used as authorizations to hire or retain people. The office is authorized two people to work as grade 7 Accountants (the expression under the word "Accountant" describes the position as General Schedule, job series number 0510, pay grade 7). If there were, for any reason, a third grade 7 Accountant in the office, that person would be in an unauthorized position and would constitute an "overhire." The third person does not have a "slot" to occupy in the office. When offices are rapidly expanding (or just being established), some supervisors may use the overhire practice to hire someone in advance of, and in anticipation that the agency personnel office will establish such a position in the near future.

There are two grade 7, three grade 9 and two grade 11 Accountant positions in this office, plus a grade 12 supervisory position. These could constitute a "career ladder" for the people in the grade 7, 9 and 11 positions; the people in this ladder may anticipate that time in grade at the grade 7, 9 and 11 positions would prepare them for promotion to positions "higher" on the career ladder when one becomes vacant. Theoretically, the work experiences they have in these positions would fulfill the kinds of work experience required of applicants for higher level positions within the office. That is, they would be assigned various tasks and responsibilities which are required by people applying for the higher graded positions. Under normal circumstances, the secretary and the two voucher examiners would not be in the career line of the Accountant positions and would not get the assignments or responsibilities to prepare them for promotion in the Accountant series.

Further, when recruiting for a new grade 11 Accountant, the job announcement might refer to the position as a

GS-0510-07/09/11 or just as a grade 11 position. In the former case, by advertising the position at three grade levels, a person could be hired at grade 7 or 9 and, within a year, if performance has been satisfactory, the person would be promoted two grades (7 to 9 or 9 to 11). From the supervisory perspective, this creates a larger applicant pool than one limited to people only qualified for grade 11. Also, when recruiting someone from outside the agency, a supervisor may actually prefer to recruit at a lower grade level. Before the new employee does the more difficult work associated with the higher grade position, a year would be spent in the lower graded position "learning the ropes" of the way the agency operates.

Figure 4.2
Hypothetical Finance Office

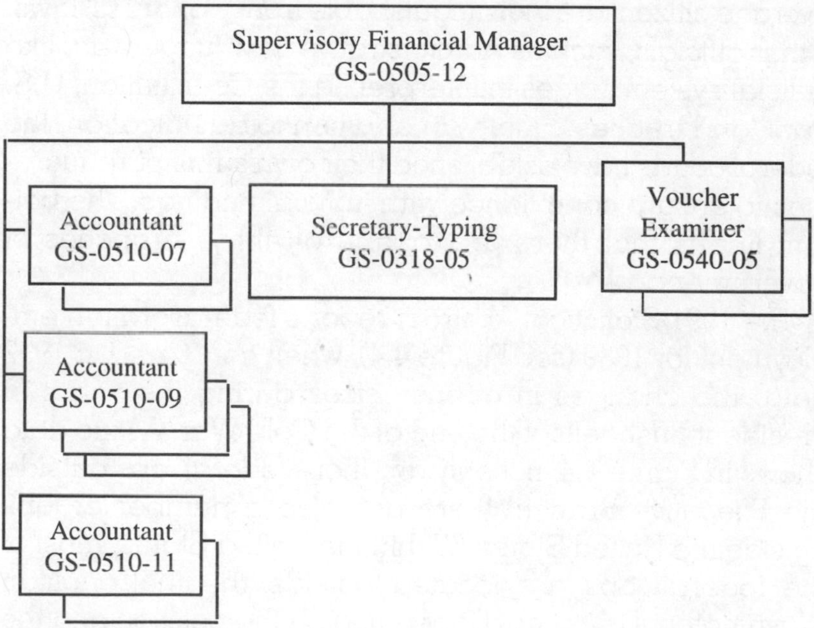

Where Are the Jobs?

Figure 4.3 shows, in general terms, the organization of the federal government. After the Constitution was ratified in the 1780s, the prevailing sentiment was that Congress (the Senate and House of Representatives) would make national laws, the Supreme Court (and later, lesser federal courts) would interpret (through their findings) the Constitution, and the Executive Branch, led by the President, would execute the laws of the land.

Two hundred years later, this neat and simple separation of powers has, to some extent, fallen by the wayside. Congress has created its own bureaucracy (including the Congressional Budget Office, General Accounting Office, and the Senate and House staffs). Various officials in the Executive Branch make rules and policies which, to the average citizen, are indistinguishable from Congress' laws. Other officials, such as Administrative Law Judges, act like judicial system judges in interpreting the Constitution, U.S. laws, and treaties. Finally, in addition to adjudication, the federal courts have established their own small bureaucracies to ensure compliance with judicial findings. The bottom line is that there are jobs in all three branches of government.

The 1991 Statistical Abstract reports federal civilian employment for 1989 (see Figure 4.4); when compared to 1992 data, the changes in agency sizes during the years of President Bush reflect the end of the Cold War. As the data shows in Figure 4.4, not only are there federal jobs outside the Executive Branch, there are also a number of jobs outside the United States. Within the United States, most of the federal jobs are located outside the metropolitan Washington, D.C. area. Depending on the position and the employing agency, federal jobs can be found anywhere from a one-person office in a small rural community to a large Federal Regional Center containing hundreds of workers from a number of different agencies.

Figure 4.3
The Federal Government

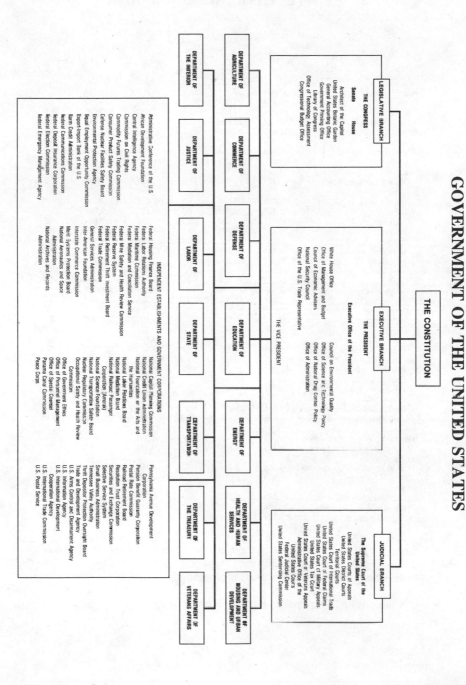

GOVERNMENT OF THE UNITED STATES

Figure 4.4
Federal Civilian Employment

AGENCY	TOTAL 1989	1992	PCT CHANGE 1989 - 1992	U.S. ONLY 1989	1992	PCT CHANGE 1989- 1992
Total, all agencies*	3,123,731	3,086,317	-1.2	2,977,621	2,965,634	-0.4
Legislative Branch, total *	37,690	38,509	2.2	37,637	38,446	2.1
Congress *	19,504	20,084	3.0	19,504	20,084	3.0
Senate	7,401	7,620	3.0	7,401	7,620	3.0
House Summary	12,090	12,446	2.9	12,090	12,446	2.9
Judicial Branch *	21,915	27,987	27.7	21,663	27,683	27.8
Supreme Court	327	353	8.0	327	353	8.0
U.S. Courts	21,588	27,551	27.6	21,336	27,247	27.7
Executive Branch, total *	3,064,126	3,018,821	-1.5	2,918,321	2,899,505	-0.6
Executive Office of the Pres. *	1,577	1,866	18.3	1,879	1,859	-1.1
Office of Management & Budget	527	586	11.2	527	586	11.2
Executive Departments	2,065,038	2,038,674	-1.3	1,939,431	1,939,260	-0.0
State	25,327	25,734	1.6	9,152	9,519	4.0
Treasury	152,548	161,951	6.2	151,517	160,805	6.1
Defense	1,075,437	982,773	-8.6	975,047	909,792	-6.7
Justice	79,667	96,927	21.7	78,217	95,173	21.7
Interior	77,545	85,260	9.9	77,175	84,847	9.9
Agriculture	122,062	128,324	5.1	120,567	126,754	5.1
Commerce	45,091	38,086	-15.5	44,366	37,197	-16.2
Labor	18,125	17,889	-1.3	18,085	17,848	-1.3
Health and Human Services	122,259	131,191	7.3	121,550	130,468	7.3
Housing and Urban Development	13,544	13,701	1.2	13,416	13,578	1.2
Transportation	65,615	70,558	7.5	65,104	70,004	7.5
Energy	17,130	20,962	22.4	17,123	20,956	22.4
Education	4,696	5,113	8.9	4,692	5,108	8.9
Veterans Affairs	245,922	260,205	5.8	243,420	257,211	5.7
Independent Agencies *	997,511	978,281	-1.9	977,323	958,386	-1.9
Environmental Protection Agency	15,590	18,196	16.7	15,572	18,173	16.7
Equal Employment Opportunity Committee	2,743	2,899	5.7	2,743	2,899	5.7
Federal Deposit Insurance Corp.	9,031	22,467	148.8	9,017	22,457	149.1
Federal Emergency Management Agency	3,048	5,632	84.8	3,038	5,465	79.9
General Services Administration	20,063	20,770	3.5	19,981	20,671	3.5
National Aeronautics & Space Administration	24,165	25,425	5.2	24,156	25,418	5.2
Nuclear Regulatory Commission	3,288	3,528	7.3	3,288	3,528	7.3
Office of Personnel Management	6,859	6,941	1.2	6,829	6,916	1.3
Small Business Administration	4,653	5,897	26.7	4,572	5,769	26.2
Tennessee Valley Authority	26,676	19,493	-26.9	26,676	19,493	-26.9
U.S. Information Agency	8,723	6,342	-27.3	4,370	4,340	-0.7

NOTES: 1989 figures are from the *1991 Statistical Abstract of the United States*, Table 529. 1992 was provided by the Office of Personnel Management from their *Monthly Report of Federal Civilian Employment (SF-113A)*.

* Includes other branches not shown separately.

Job Announcements

You have a freshly-typed, professional-quality resume which lists your educational and military background, employment history, and other skills you have. You decide you want to work for the U.S. Marshals Service, so you mail the resume to the nearest office, asking to be considered for an entry level position. If you are lucky, you will soon receive a letter indicating the error of your ways. You cannot submit resumes or applications without reference to a specific job announcement.

The federal hiring process is fairly standard, and rigid. First, an agency will publish an announcement that a vacancy exists. Next, there will be a period, as short as a few days or as long as two weeks or longer, during which applications for the vacancy will be accepted. Any applications **must** address a specific vacancy (usually, only one vacancy can be identified in an application packet). After reviewing the application packet, the applicant is either certified qualified for the position and referred to the hiring activity, or rejected for any of several reasons. Sometimes, agencies maintain lists of applicants for certain jobs comprised of applicants who were declared qualified but not selected. If, at a later time, a similar position opens in the agency, people on the applicant supply list are usually sent a copy of the new announcement and invited to apply. Time is given to complete and submit a new application, tied to the new vacancy announcement.

When an organization or agency needs to fill a vacancy, it will typically publish **a vacancy announcement**.[4] Sam-

---

[4]*Federal Career Opportunities*, published every two weeks by the Federal Research Service, P.O. Box 1059, Vienna, VA 22183, is in many employment offices, personnel offices, public libraries. An extensive list of federal job announcements, both U.S.-based and overseas, is in each issue.

ples of announcements are in Appendix F. There are several important pieces of information on an announcement. The first is the announcement number (ANN. NO.). Every sheet of paper in your application *must* contain your name, social security number, and the announcement number. The next most important item is the closing date. Applications received after this date are usually not accepted. Ideally, you want to have the application arrive a few days before the closing date. As will be shown in Chapter Six, this gives you time to call back and ensure that you've provided everything needed to evaluate your application and give you time to make any last minute changes.

An announcement also has a section describing who is qualified to apply for the vacancy. Positions are sometimes limited to people who have employment **status** with the federal government. That is, only someone who is currently a federal employee or who has employment rights can apply for the job. Sometimes status will be even further limited to people in a specific geographic area or to people who already work for the agency. In the *Federal Career Opportunities* listing of vacancies, such limited positions are marked with an "(S)."

Other sections of the announcement describe applicant qualifications, including what kinds of education and specialized or general work experience is required. As shown in Figure 4.5, the importance of general experience, education, and specialized experience changes with the grade level of a job. For lower-graded jobs, such as those below GS-9, general experience and education often suffice. At higher levels, especially above GS-11, even higher levels of education sometimes cannot substitute for specialized experience.

Specialized experience refers to work experience which is directly related to the position in the announcement. Usually, this is expressed as work comparable to

Figure 4.5
Education/Experience Mix

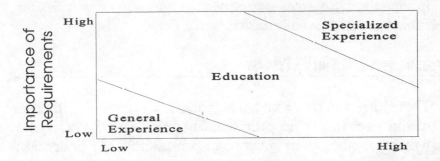

Target Job Grade Level

that done at the next lower grade level. A GS-11 job, for example, may require a year's experience doing the kind of tasks done at grade GS-9 (or -10) for that job. The specialized experience section of an announcement will typically list three or more kinds of specialized experience required.

When applications are reviewed, one of three things will happen to the application. First, the applicant may be rated qualified for the opening and referred to the hiring activity. That is, the personnel office has reviewed the application and given it enough points to qualify for referral. Some agencies, like the Department of State, put all qualified applicants on a **register** or applicant supply list. Successful candidates are placed in rank-order by their relative competitiveness on a register for an eighteen month period. Offers of employment are made to the most competitive candidates from the top of the register, as openings become available. Naturally, if an application is near the bottom of the list, as other, more qualified applicants enter the register, they are placed higher on the list and are more likely to be offered a job. The third possibility is that an applicant is declared not qualified. Usual sticking points are educational deficiencies or insufficient experience. In a few cases, applicants can contact the personnel office and correct misunderstandings or supply additional information. See the recommendations in Chapter Six for making a successful application.

Organizations in the Hiring Process

There are a number of organizations with responsibilities in the Federal hiring process. They can all affect, in one way or another, your success in completing an application for a federal job.

Office of Personnel Management (OPM)

The Office of Personnel Management is a separate agency in the Executive Branch and is responsible for establishing government-wide standards for hiring, firing, promotions, equal employment opportunities, and a host of other personnel functions. In the past, OPM played a crucial role in the hiring process as the initial point of contact for someone seeking a federal job.

Today, OPM plays an "honest broker" role in the hiring process. OPM establishes government-wide guidelines and procedures to be used by agency personnel offices to manage aspects of the personnel process. These general guidelines and procedures help standardize the ways jobs are defined, how people are recruited, what criteria are used to evaluate job applicants, and what an agency must do to ensure that equal employment opportunities are provided. One example of such a guideline is the standards used to evaluate applicants for GS positions (X-118 Qualification Standards). These standards help a personnel specialist review job applicants' backgrounds and rate their suitability for a vacancy.

OPM is responsible for several other products which

may be of interest to someone seeking a federal job:

- *Handbook of Occupational Groups and Series:* This helps the separate agencies classify positions, determine what grade is appropriate for the kind of work and responsibility in the position;

- *Handbook X-118 or Qualification Standards Handbook:* This describes the criteria to be used by agency personnel specialists to rate a job applicant's background and experience; standard "work performed" lists for each grade of each GS job (grades 1 through 15) are in this handbook;

- *Career America Connection (912-757-3000):* This is a phone answering service available 24 hours a day, seven days a week, that provides information about current employment and career opportunities, special programs for students, veterans, and people with disabilities, the Presidential Management Intern Program, and salaries and benefits.

- *Federal Job Opportunities Bulletin Board (912-757-3100):* This and four regional electronic bulletin boards provide information about open examinations and job vacancy announcements worldwide. Anyone with a computer equipped with a modem can contact one of these information sources (see Appendix C for more information).

- *Federal Occupational and Career Information System (FOCIS):* This is a computer program which describes work in the federal service, helps users determine positions for which they might be eligible (including job series and grade), and identifies where (geographically and by agency) such positions exist. Copies are available at federal employment information centers (see below) and in some state employment offices and larger city libraries.

The Office of Personnel Management consists of the Central Office or Office Headquarters, the Washington Area Service Center (WASC), five Regional Offices, and the Federal Employment Information Centers. The Central Office in Washington, D.C. takes the lead in establishing federal policies for federal personnel management. This means they make policy on recruitment, examinations, leader development, training, administration of pay plans, job classification, personnel investigations, and employee evaluation procedures. They also administer employee retirement and insurance programs and advise agencies in labor relations and affirmative action.

The WASC and the five Regional Offices ensure that OPM programs and policies are followed in their areas (the WASC covers the metropolitan Washington, D.C. area, Atlantic overseas, and some worldwide activities). Daily administration within each region is conducted by one of the six or more Area Offices subordinate to the Regional Office. Area Offices handle the distribution of job information within an Area, and manage recruitment and examining in their Areas.

A Federal Employment Information Center is usually contained in each Area Office. FEICs help people seeking federal employment. A job seeker may visit a FEIC and obtain job announcements, application forms, advice on how to apply for work, and how to be tested for federal jobs. (Please note, however, that some FEICs are "self service" and do not provide advice to someone seeking a federal job, and many are shutting down or consolidating with other offices.) Appendix E lists OPM Regional and Area Offices, FEICs, and the WASC.

Federal Agencies

Agency personnel offices, using policy and procedure guidance from OPM, play key roles in the personnel process. Agencies establish positions by securing funding for a position, determining the appropriate pay plan, job series and grade for the position, recruiting applicants for the position, evaluating and ranking applicants, and "in-processing" newly hired people (assisting new employees in selecting insurance and retirement plans, apprising them of their rights, preparing personnel records' files and so on). Agencies also manage their own RIFs. While smaller federal agencies may only have one personnel office, larger activities such as the Department of Defense, have established personnel offices throughout the United States and overseas. The Department of Defense also has created, at large or centrally-located military installations, "One Stop Job Shops" which, much like the FEICs, help people get federal jobs (primarily in the Department of Defense). A One Stop Job Shop also often includes personnel trained to assist an applicant in getting a federal job. Also, One Stop Job Shops list Defense Department positions not listed elsewhere, especially those positions funded by non-appropriated funds (NAF). Post or Base Exchanges, libraries, morale/welfare/recreation positions and other activities at military installations may have one or more positions which are funded by money raised primarily at the installation through Officers' and Noncommissioned Officers' Clubs, golf courses, and other morale, welfare or recreational activities at the installation (that is, the position is not paid from Congressional appropriations but from locally generated income, hence the term non-appropriated).

Federal agencies play another role in the application process. While the OPM establishes, in the *X-118 Handbooks*, guidelines for evaluating job applicants, federal agencies may create additional guidelines. The *X-118 Handbook*, for example, establishes in general terms the education and work experience someone needs to become a system accountant. The agency may establish additional requirements unique to the kinds of work a system accountant does for the agency (for example, requiring experience with a particular computer system). General Schedule positions for which single agency standards have been published are marked with an asterisk in Appendix E.

State Employment Offices

Employment offices in many states play a vital role in helping people find and apply for federal jobs. State employment offices typically will have a listing of federal job openings within the state. Some state employment offices also have copies of *X-118 Handbooks* available for people to examine when preparing applications. Finally, employment offices in some states offer training seminars to help people prepare for interviews, or otherwise market themselves for jobs. These confidence-building exercises can be particularly useful for people who plan on federal jobs but have not had military experience or prior federal employment.

Public Libraries

A final resource organization for the process of applying for federal jobs is the local library. Public libraries in or near metropolitan areas and university or college libraries will often have copies of the *X-118 Handbooks* available. Many also subscribe to *Federal Career Opportunities* or *Federal Jobs Digest*, two publications which list federal vacancies around the world. While not all federal jobs are listed in these publications, they do provide a host of employment opportunities for people seeking federal jobs.

A large library will typically have other assets which can provide the kinds of background information needed to successfully complete an application packet. They may, for instance, have a copy of the FOCIS computer program to help people determine which career in federal service is right for them, or computer programs which help prepare application forms (i.e., programs which make professional-looking SF 171s or OF 612s).

Summary

Several important points were presented here about the federal job process. First, the focus of federal employment is on **positions**; a position is like an open box within an office or activity. The box is defined in terms of the tasks required by people in the position, which position super-vises the position, and which positions it supervises, in turn. These characteristics of the position help personnel specialists assign a job series and grade (such as a Criminal Investigator, GS-1811-09) to the position.

Secondly, there is a wide variety of positions available in the federal government, ranging from Wage Grade Laborer positions through Senior Executive Service positions. Further, there are opportunities throughout the country and even overseas, and across all three branches of government.

Finally, there are a number of agencies involved, in one way or another, with the process of getting a federal job. OPM and the agencies set standards for work. Standards may require that tasks X, Y and Z be performed by a grade 7 position; and anyone applying for a grade 9 position in the same job series must have a year's experience doing those three tasks. A number of organizations, including state employment offices, local libraries, and Federal Employment Information Centers, can help you find vacancies, get copies of the announcements, and complete an application for the vacancy.

This chapter has reviewed working for the federal government. We have provided the basis for the next chapter's examination of federal careers in law enforcement.

Chapter 5

STARTING A CAREER
IN LAW ENFORCEMENT

There are over a hundred combinations of job series and agencies which represent entry level jobs in law enforcement. Because of this diversity, we will discuss just a few examples of the job series and agencies involved in law enforcement. To a large extent, these examples show what can be expected in most of the other job series and agencies.[1]

---

[1]*Federal Jobs in Law Enforcement*, John W. Warner, Jr., New York: Prentice Hall, Inc., 1992, has thumbnail sketches of most of the agencies engaged in federal law enforcement. Some of the addresses for further information are not current and the focus is more on what the *agency* does than on the position and what the *position* requires, and there is little coverage of what one does in entry level positions.

The Scope of Work

Investigator (GS-1810) or Criminal Investigator (GS-1811) positions are the most common law enforcement positions in the federal government. Agency Inspectors General (IG) use these positions to prevent and detect fraud, waste and abuse in agency programs and operations. IGs will normally do this by supervising audits, inspections and investigations, and by providing plans to improve economy, efficiency and effectiveness. An investigation can look at agency employees, people affected by the agency's programs (for example, people receiving the benefits of a program), and the contractors supplying the agency. The results of these investigations sometimes lead to indictments and prosecution, and can lead to fines, prison sentences, or other criminal, civil or administrative penalties. The scope of such investigations may range from simple fraud to the waste of millions of dollars in an agency. Typically, these positions involve travel to various offices or organizations under review.

In the Department of Defense, the IG stresses the importance of crime prevention through the use of crime prevention surveys, vulnerability assessments (i.e., identifying aspects of a program which are vulnerable to fraud, waste or abuse), internal control reviews, and fraud awareness training. In the National Aeronautics and Space Administration IG Office, attention is given to violations of laws relating to falsified contractual documents (payrolls, deviations from contract specifications, and so forth). Criminal Investigators are given wide-ranging audit and investigative responsibility to pursue their examinations of DOD programs. These positions usually begin at General Schedule grade GS-5 or GS-7 and the career path can progress through the Senior Executive Service level, depending on the agency.

Investigators in the Defense Investigative Service conduct personnel security investigations of people to determine their suitability for a position of trust. These background investigations examine a person's background and character and investigators have to prepare Reports of Investigations of subjects. In the Naval Criminal Investigative Service (NCIS), Criminal Investigators/Special Agents participate in general crime investigations (such as felonies on Navy or Marine bases), in counter-drug programs off bases, and investigations of white collar crimes affecting the Navy/Marine Corps and their personnel. One third of NCIS personnel engage in counterintelligence work against terrorists and hostile intelligence services. In the DIS, Investigator positions begin at GS-5 and continue through GS-11. Criminal Investigator/Special Agent positions in the NCIS begin at grade GS-7 and go through GS-12.

The Department of State has positions for Special Agents/Diplomatic Security Officers beginning at Foreign Service Grade FP-6. These positions are responsible for the security of Foreign Service personnel, property, and sensitive information throughout the world. They are also responsible for the security of American and foreign dignitaries. Major activities include protective services, background and criminal investigations, management of security programs for Foreign Service posts, and administrative, training and liaison duties. Domestic assignments usually involve protecting foreign dignitaries, conducting background investigations, and criminal investigations to protect the integrity of passport and visa documents. Overseas, this position is one of security officer at a diplomatic or Consular office. Both domestic and overseas postings can involve considerable travel.

The Securities and Exchange Commission (SEC) has a different type of law enforcement position, with work similar to that found in the Justice Department, the FBI, and in many other federal agencies: the General Attorney (GS-905). An SEC General Attorney enforces several laws pertaining to securities (stocks, bonds and other instruments). Duties include investigative hearings to get testimony and documentary evidence, preparing reports of legal issues involved in a case, participating in civil suits and administrative proceedings to resolve cases, and sometimes working with U.S. Attorneys to pursue criminal violations of securities' laws. General Attorney positions usually begin around GS-11 and progress through higher grades to GM-15 or even SES.

A final example of a law enforcement position is that of Game Warden (GS-1802). Game wardens, Park Service and Forest Service Rangers, Fish and Wildlife Service Agents and others all have responsibility for protecting fish and wildlife resources and controlling human activities to ensure effective management of these resources. Wardens enforce local, state and federal laws pertaining to the use of the natural environment. This can and often does involve the full range of complex and difficult law enforcement activities to include surveillance, participation in raids, interviewing witnesses, interrogating suspects, searching for and seizing evidence, seizing contraband, securing crime scenes, securing and serving search warrants, making apprehensions, inspecting records and documents, and assisting U.S. Attorneys in preparing civil or criminal cases. Wardens, Rangers and Agents work on all types of federal lands (as well as off shore), from individual military installations to huge national parks. Jobs begin at grade GS-5 or -7, usually, and advance through grade GS-12.

Qualifications

Entry level federal jobs require a mix of education, general experience and specialized experience (as shown in

Chapter 4). Generally, the lower the grade of the job, the less important the role of education and specialized experience. GS-5 and GS-7 jobs, for example, normally emphasize general experience, such as ability to communicate orally and in writing, supervisory recommendations on ability to follow orders, and ability to work with people. Often, some college (especially college courses related to the work done by the position) can substitute for general experience. Entry at higher grades (GS-9 or GS-10) often requires graduate education or college graduation with a high grade point average and opportunities to substitute education for experience lessen. At higher grades, sometimes college education cannot substitute for at least a year of specialized experience (i.e., one must have spent at least a year doing the work of the next lower grade).

General experience for a Criminal Investigator with the DOD IG means progressively more responsible experience which demonstrated:

- Ability to work or deal effectively with individuals or groups at the highest level of an organization ;

- Initiative, ingenuity, resourcefulness, and judgement required to collect, assemble, develop and analyze information;

- Ability to plan logical outlines and write clear, complete and concise reports;

- Willingness and ability to successfully accept and perform progressively more responsible work.

A year of specialized experience is also required at GS-7 (there are some substitutions for education); specialized experiences include:

- Ability to think and act logically and objectively;

- Ability to analyze complex sets of records, gather facts and evidence, interview suspects/witnesses, and make sound recommendations;

- Skill in planning assigned work by defining objectives, outlining steps, setting milestones, and executing plans;

- Skill in organizing facts, analyzing issues, and preparing reports;

- Ability to gain the cooperation and confidence of others; and

- Knowledge of criminal investigation techniques and procedures, obtaining and serving warrants, making arrests, searches and seizures, securing evidence, testifying in trials, and general court procedures.

These basically are required in all entry level law enforcement positions in the federal government. The language changes from agency to agency, but these illustrate the qualifications, **in general terms**. As noted earlier, the best indication of what is required for a job will be the job announcement, standards for the position and the next lower position (either qualification standards or a position description).

The DOD IG also requires a pre-employment physical and urinalysis, and limits the age of applicants to 21 through 34 years of age (with some limited exceptions). Criminal Investigators with NASA's IG or the Defense Investigative Service further must have a bachelor's degree at the GS-5 level and either a high grade point average or post graduate education in a law enforcement related discipline.

Diplomatic Security Officers with the State Department need both a college degree and one year of specialized experience for the entry level FP-6 position. Specialized experience here is virtually the same as that with a DOD IG but includes physical security of people and places.

General Attorneys with the SEC are required to have both a law degree and bar membership (law clerks may be hired but they must get bar membership within fourteen months). As might be expected, specialized experience requirements for an attorney position differ from those for investigator positions. Knowledge of federal rules of civil procedure and rules of evidence are required, as well as trial and pre-trial procedures, and, for SEC attorneys, applicants must be familiar with the securities business, accounting, financial analysis, corporate finances, and corporate practices in general.

Investigator positions, Special Agent positions, Game Wardens, Rangers, and similar positions also usually require applicants to be physically fit. Most federal law enforcement positions have this requirement when the conditions of work require work outdoors, whether in physical security or investigating a site.

Finally, given the nature of law enforcement jobs, applicants must also undergo rigorous background checks, often must be U.S. citizens, must be able to obtain a secret or top secret clearance, must submit financial disclosure statements, often must be proficient in firearms and other devices, and generally expect closer scrutiny than a clerk typist might encounter.

Special Hiring Programs

Federal organizations have made significant progress in implementing programs to diversify the kinds of applicants selected for entry level positions. One of the oldest and strongest programs is the Ten Point Veteran Preference (see Appendix I for detailed information). This program improves employment prospects for veterans who have a service-related disability or received the Purple Heart, the spouse of a disabled veteran, or the widow/widower of a veteran. The Veterans Readjustment Appointment Act is another special hiring program for some veterans who served during the period 1964 through 1975.

Agencies which require a four year college degree for their entry level positions typically send recruiters to historically Black colleges and universities. Such agencies will also normally have Student Trainee positions (GS-X99 - such as GS-1899, Investigation Student Trainee or GS-999, Legal Occupations Student Trainee). These may involve summer work or part time work during the normal academic year in the junior and senior years. Upon graduation, student trainees become eligible for vacancies in the job family (such as the 1800 job family). The State Department IG, for example, may offer an entry level Criminal Investigator position to a student intern/trainee upon successful completion of the college degree program.

Starting a Career

Creation of a successful application packet is the first step in beginning any career in the federal government. Chapter Three described how job announcements are used to solicit applications. A typical application packet for a federal job may include the following items (the ones listed are required of almost every applicant):

- SF 171, OF 612 or a federal style resume;

- Supervisory evaluation;

- DD 214 or SF 15 for veterans' preference;

- College transcript;

- (Race and Sex) Background Survey;

- SF 50 showing status (if claiming status);

- Supplemental Information Sheets.

Detailed help on completing an application packet can be found elsewhere (see the list of resources at the end of Chapter Six). The most important thing to remember when completing an application packet is that the first person to review your application may know very little about the job. He or she will, in most instances, grade your application by comparing it with standards for the job. If you want to make a successful application, you need to ensure that what you say can be clearly and unambiguously compared to the standards. Examples of position standards for some entry level law enforcement jobs are shown in Appendix G.

When describing your background, you need not limit it to civilian work experiences. Obviously, many tasks performed in the military can be described and should apply. "Cleaning and maintaining small arms," most basic infantry skills, and even work as a duty officer should be listed and described (tell what you did as a duty officer, for example, and how many times a month you did this). Volunteer work with clubs or churches also can be listed. If you helped a church set up and conduct a clothing sale, for example, describe the tasks you performed. All these can contribute points to your "generalized experience," if not to your "specialized experience!"

Submitting the application packet is also not just a matter of typing and mailing your forms. See the next chapter for a detailed action plan. Remember that your application packet will be the first thing a hiring official sees about you. The more well-organized and efficiently you communicate yourself, the stronger the impression you make on the hiring official. Having a sound and tightly organized plan of applying for a job helps keep your application organized and efficient!

After a personnel specialist determines whether an applicant is qualified for an entry level position, the applicant might be placed on a register (see Chapter 4) or might begin a series of "tests," including an oral interview, background screen, urinalysis test, and physical or medical exam. These are not normally encountered by people applying for federal jobs but are required given the nature of federal law enforcement work. Failure of any of these "tests" can result in disqualification.

The start of an entry level federal career in law enforcement almost always involves some time spent in training. The FBI Academy on the Marine Corps Base at Quantico, VA and the Department of the Treasury's Federal Law Enforcement Training Center (FLETC) at Glynco, GA are encountered during the first year of many newly-hired officers. The FBI Academy provides training in behavioral sciences and forensic sciences, weapons training, legal instruction, and training in economic and financial crimes. The FLETC provides basic training to Criminal Investigators and uniformed police officers who are authorized to carry firearms and make arrests. Training is also offered in behavioral sciences, fundamentals of law, financial fraud, forensics, physical security, driver and marine classes, and weapons training. Also, many federal agencies have training courses, from three days in length to several weeks in length, covering topics applicable to law enforcement officers within the agency. The Defense Investigative Service, for example, has a four week basic course in Richmond, VA for new or inexperienced agents on policies and procedures of Personnel Security Investigations.

New FBI Special Agents spend sixteen weeks at the FBI

Academy before being assigned to a field office, while new agents of the Naval Criminal Investigative Service spend the same amount of time in the Basic Agent Course at the FLETC. This includes the ten week Criminal Investigators' Course taught by FLETC and a six week NCIS course taught by NCIS staff and covering topics specific to the Service. There is also a two month course at FLETC for Criminal Investigators in Inspector General activities.

Upon completion of any required training, the newly hired Investigator or Agent is usually sent to a field office (especially in the larger federal organizations) and may get additional training during the first year or so on the job. Also, after about twelve through eighteen months on the job, people who have successfully performed their work with the agency are often give a promotion, such as from a GS-5 or GS-7 to a GS-7 or GS-9.

Following this first year, further career development with most federal agencies requires additional training, increasingly more responsible work, and often rotation to other offices. As more experience in the agency's work is gained, the prospects for promotion to higher grades improves, and the individual has launched a federal career in law enforcement.

Chapter 6

THE APPLICATION ACTION PLAN AND CAREER RESOURCES

This last chapter reviews an action plan for pursuing a federal career in law enforcement. Information from preceding chapters is used to help you plan and execute a sequence of steps to prepare, submit, and track an application packet. A checklist version of the plan is provided in Appendix H. This chapter gives brief explanations of each part of the checklist and also describes the log sheet (in Appendix I) for managing your federal job search. A strong application packet requires:

- A **target** (job series *and* grade);
- **Information** about the target;
- An **action plan** to reach the target.

I. LIST YOUR ASSETS

A. Identify, in general terms, your:

1. **Educational background:** locate or get copies of all diplomas, certificates, and college transcripts. For some positions, you may need to have copies of course contents (from college catalogs) to justify educational experiences which are not readily apparent from the course titles on transcripts. You may need to prepare lists of relevant college or post-high school courses, on-the-job training, and short term training.

2. **Previous paid and unpaid work/efforts:** make two lists covering the past ten years. One list will have your paid work, starting with the most recent job and working back through time. You will need start and end dates, highest pay, job series and grade if a federal job, and a point of contact, phone, and address. The second list shows all outside activities, volunteer work, and unpaid jobs in which you demonstrated skills appropriate to your target job. Recently discharged veterans may be eligible to get DD Form 2586, "Verification of Military Experience and Training," which lists their job skills and experiences acquired while on active duty which may apply to civilian jobs (including federal jobs).[1]

---

[1]Call 800-258-8638 or write to PRC, Inc., Attn: VMET, G-3.03, 12001 Sunrise Valley Drive, Reston, VA, 22091. Discharged/released veterans who separated after 1 October 1990, reservists who have served 180 consecutive days of active duty since that date, and active duty military members within 180 days of their projected and approved separation may be eligible.

B. **Identify, in general terms, where you want to work:** Consider where you want to work (what cities or states appeal to you). Check Appendix C and find the Federal Employment Information Center (FEIC) serving the area where you want to work. This is the first place to contact for job announcements, examination announcements, and information about your application package.

C. **What federal organizations appeal to you?** Do you have any interest in working for specific federal agencies? Are you interested in work for Congress or the Courts, or independent agencies and commissions? The cost of obtaining job announcements can be significantly reduced if you limit the number of organizations which interest you. Also, perhaps the mission of certain federal organizations appeals to you more than the missions of other organizations.

II. IDENTIFY JOBS AND GRADES FOR WHICH YOU ARE ELIGIBLE:

A. **Use FOCIS:** Check Federal Employment Information Centers, state employment offices, and local libraries for a copy of this computer program. This can be used by anyone to quickly find jobs which might interest you or help you narrow the list of jobs to which you might apply.

B. **Get advice from OPM or state employment counselors:** If FOCIS is unavailable or if more help is needed, counselors at FEICs, some federal personnel offices within departments, and state employment counselors can help you narrow the list of jobs for which you might apply.

C. **Scan appendices in this book (job series and the general qualification standards):** Appendix E has a comprehensive list of General Schedule (GS) jobs. If a GS job series sounds attractive, Appendix G lists general education and experience requirements for most GS jobs.

III. FOCUS ON THE REQUIREMENTS FOR TARGET JOBS:

After you have identified one or more target jobs, agencies and parts of the country where you would like to work, contact FEICs in the appropriate area (or, if you have a computer and modem, contact the Federal Jobs Hotline) for further information.

A. **Identify any required exams:**

1. **Call nearest OPM for test dates and sites:** Ask whether any exams are required for the target job; get the name and any information available about any exams. College place-ment offices and large post offices will also have examination announcements.

2. **Check libraries for hints, sample questions, or copies of old exams:** Some libraries have information about federal exams; ask them about exams for your target job.

B. **Review X-118 standards and agency-made standards:**

1. **Determine whether your assets qualify you for the target job:** Check Appendix G for the qualification standards for major groups of GS jobs. If more information is needed, check the position classification standards for the series which interests you. At this time, be sure to check the job's "Status" requirement. Do you meet this requirement? (For example, if the "Status" is "Federal employees," are you currently a federal employee?)

2. **Does the target series/grade appeal to you:** (Does it seem to offer what you want in terms of work and pay)?

3. **Are you almost qualified for other series or grades?** Check similar jobs in the same job family (or other families that interest you) and check other grades in the interesting jobs. Do the standards indicate whether you are qualified? Can you qualify by taking one or a few post-high school course(s)?

IV. GET CURRENT JOB ANNOUNCEMENTS FROM:

A. **OPM's FEICs or the *Career America Connection*** listed in Appendix C.

B. **Agency personnel offices** should be checked if you want to work for a specific agency. The FEIC can provide you with the address for the nearest personnel office for the desired agency. The central or headquarters office for many agencies is listed in Appendix D. If interested in working for the Department of Defense, check the nearest military base to determine whether there is a "One Stop Job Shop" at the base or post.

C. **State employment offices** usually carry recent federal announcements within the state.

D. *Federal Career Opportunities/Federal Jobs Digest* list recently announced vacancies, as well as open and continuous hire positions. Also check the *Federal Times*, a weekly newspaper.

E. **Federal Job Opportunities Bulletin Boards** usually carry recent federal announcements grouped by geographic region and job family.

V. BEGIN PREPARING THE APPLICATION PACKET

A. **Get *X-118 Qualification Standards* for the target job**: Use the job series number and grade and contact an FEIC, state employment office or local library for the qualification standards. Note that qualification standards for GS job families are in Appendix G.

B. **If more information is needed, get *Position Classification Standards* for the target job** from a FEIC or state employment office.

C. **Examine the announcement: Are additional forms needed?** Note all the other forms listed on the announcement. Some key forms are in Appendix I. Current federal employees in need of a recent SF 50 should contact their servicing personnel office.

D.   If not already prepared, make a "master" SF 171/OF 612 for the target series and grade. A "master" form is an OF 612 or SF 171 application form which is only partially completed. On an SF 171, leave blank the following blocks: 1, 11, 12, 23, 48 and 49. On OF 612, leave blank blocks: 1-3, 8, 9, and 18. When you apply for a specific vacancy, you can make a photo copy and then complete the black blocks targeted at the specific vacancy.

E.   Call for more information about the vacancy: There will be a phone number and point of contact (POC) on the announcement; record this number and name on the Log Sheet (Appendix I) and contact the POC for more information about the position (is it still open, does "closing date" on the announcement mean the date the application packet has to be in their hands or is the closing date the last acceptable postmark date on the packet; what is the schedule for filling the position; can you call the hiring official for more information about the job).

VI.   PREPARE A "MAIL-IN" PACKET

A.   Make a clear copy of the master SF 171 or OF 612 and complete any unfilled blocks,

including block 1 and your signature and date:

B. **Prepare the supplemental forms (race and sex surveys, SF 15, KSA sheets, etc.)**

C. **Make a photo copy of the completed packet:** If not using a computer to make your application packet, after making a master, make at least one good, clear photo copy of the master. This copy will be completed and mailed in your application packet. **You also need to make a copy of the mail-in packet.** If your packet is lost, you will need to rush another copy to the POC. At the very least, copy those pages in the mail-in copy that have blanks which you completed (example, the first, second and last pages of the SF 171, have blocks that are blank on the master but are completed on the mail-in copy).

D. **Mail the application packet and complete a log record:** using the Log Sheet in Appendix I. Make every effort to mail the packet at least a week before the closing date. Some offices require the packets **postmarked by the closing date;** some require the packets **in their hands by the closing date.** Use special delivery services (one-day, two-day, etc.) and try to allow at least two days of slack (that is, plan to get your packet to the personnel office at least two days before the vacancy closes).

VII. FOLLOW-THROUGH

A. Call the POC a few days later and ask:

1. **Whether the packet arrived:** Try to call *before* the closing date of the announcement; you should have planned to get the packet to the personnel office at least two days before the closing date (see 6.D., above). If they do not have your packet, you may still have time to ship another copy before the deadline.

2. **Has anything changed regarding that vacancy:** Was the closing date extended? Was the position closed? Log any changes into your Log Sheet.

3. **What timetable will be followed in rating the applications and sending ratings to hiring officials:** When does the POC expect to have the packets ranked and when will the packets be sent to the hiring official? Note this schedule in the Log Sheet. Also ask for a good time to call back for the status of your application.[2]

---

[2]Recruiters sometimes have scores of applications to process and each call interrupts their work. You need to call only at the key steps in the review process to track your application and the recruitment specialists can tell you the best time to make such calls.

B. Based on the timetable given by the POC, call later to find out if you were rated:

1. **If you were not rated, ask why not:** The purpose of this question is not to chastise the recruiting official but to find out why your application was not ranked and forwarded to the hiring official. This is a learning experience; your application is being critiqued by a pro; use his or her recommendations to make your next submission even better. On your Log Sheet, note the date of your call and the name of the person with whom you talked.

2. **If your application was misread, ask to appeal the rating:** If you believe that your packet was misread by the recruiting official, ask to discuss why you believe a mistake was made and ask whether something can be done to put you back in the running. Again, you do *not* want to be angry with the recruiting official; he or she may have had to process dozens of applications and may have made an honest mistake that can be corrected to your satisfaction. If not, you can still use this as a learning experience to apply when you submit future application packets.

3. **Again ask for timetable and other information about this vacancy:** If you can resubmit a corrected packet for this vacancy, ask the recruiting official for a deadline **and meet**

those deadlines! Note the deadlines on your Log Sheet.

C. **If rated, call back every two weeks and ask:**

1. **Has the application gone to the hiring activity.**

2. **Has anything changed regarding the vacancy:** Record the date of each call, the name of the person who talked to you, and the information you got from the call. Normally, a personnel official will not call you about changes in the status of a vacancy. If your packet was not rated and sent to a hiring official, you probably will not be notified until someone was hired, so you need to regularly check the status of your application and log the information in your Log Sheet.

D. **If not selected, call the POC and ask why:** Try to find out what would have made your application stronger.

E. **Update the log records:** Close your Log Sheet by describing why your application was not successful and make any necessary changes in your master application.

Resources

The following resources include valuable information for assisting you with your federal job search. Appendix D lists the headquarters offices of federal organizations which often have vacancies in law enforcement. Most of these resources are available directly from the publisher or through Impact Publications. For your convenience, please refer to the "Career Resource" section at the end of this book which includes those resources available directly through Impact Publications.

JOB HOTLINES

Career America Connection: (912) 757-3000, lists federal jobs and has forms and announcements. Requires a touch tone phone.

GOVERNMENT PUBLICATIONS

All federal government publications may be purchased from US Government Book Stores (usually found in cities with FEICs) or from:

> The Superintendent of Documents
> U.S. Government Printing Office
> Washington, D.C. 20402-9325
> (202) 512-1800

FEDERAL JOB STANDARDS

Federal job standards such as qualification or classification standards, may be obtained from:

> U.S. Office of Personnel Management
> Staffing Service Center
> Career Entry Group
> 4685 Log Cabin Drive
> Macon, GA 31298-0001
> (912) 744-2168

JOB LISTINGS/SUBSCRIPTION SERVICES

Federal Career Opportunities
P.O. Box 1059
Vienna, VA 22183
(703) 281-0200
Biweekly

Federal Jobs Digest
325 Pennsylvania Ave., SE
Washington, D.C. 20003
(800) 543-3000
Biweekly

Federal Times
6885 Commercial Drive
Springfield, VA, 22159
Weekly Newspaper
(703) 750-9000

BOOKS AND CATALOGS

Damp, Dennis V., **The Book of U.S. Government Jobs**, 1992, D-Amp Publications.

Government Directory of Addresses and Telephone Numbers, 1993, Omnigraphics.

Hammer, Hy, **The Civil Service Handbook**, Arco/Prentice-Hall.

Hammer, Hy, **Complete Guide to U.S. Civil Service Jobs**, Arco/Prentice-Hall.

Hammer, Hy, **General Test Practice for 101 U.S. Jobs**, Arco/Prentice-Hall.

"Jobs and Careers for the 1990's" a free flyer listing resources to help someone seeking *any* kind of employment, from Impact Publications, 9104-N Manassas Drive, Manassas Park, VA 22111, (703) 361-7300 (fax 703-335-9486).

Krannich, Ronald L. and Caryl Rae, **Directory of Federal Jobs and Employers**, 1996, Impact Publications, see address above.

Krannich, Ronald L. and Caryl Rae, **The Complete Guide to Public Employment**, 1995, Impact Publications, see address above.

Krannich, Ronald L. and Caryl Rae, **Find a Federal Job Fast! How to Cut the Red Tape and Get Hired**, 1995, Impact Publications, see address above.

Kraus, Krandall, **How to Get a Federal Job**, 1989, Facts on File.

Lauber, Daniel, **The Government Job Finder**, 1993, Planning/Communications.

Smith, Russ, **Federal Applications That Get Results**, 1996, Impact Publications, see address above.

U.S. Office of Personnel Management, **X-118 Qualification Standards Handbook**, TS-230, March 1990, order from The Superintendent of Documents (above).

U.S. Office of Personnel Management, **Position Classification Standards for the ____ Series GS-_**, TS-(various numbers), various dates, order from The Superintendent of Documents (above) the standards for the target job with which you are most interested.

Waelde, David, *How to Get a Federal Job*, 1989, FEDHELP Publications.

Warner, John W., *Federal Jobs in Law Enforcement*, 1992, Arco/Prentice-Hall.

Wood, Patricia B., *The 171 Reference Book*, 1991, Workbooks, Inc.

Wood, Patricia B., *Promote Yourself*, 1991, Workbooks, Inc.

COMPUTER SOFTWARE PROGRAMS

FOCIS—Federal Occupational and Career Information System, U.S. Office of Personnel Management.

Quick and Easy Federal Job Kits, DataTech. (contact Impact Publications for both DOS and Windows versions. Available in four versions—individuals (1 user), family (2 users), office (8 users), and professional (unlimited users).

COMPUTER BULLETIN BOARDS

Federal Job Opportunities Bulletin Boards, provided by the U.S.. Office of Personnel Management, require a computer and a modem to access job announcements. See Appendix C for a list of the boards and connection parameters.

APPENDICES

Appendix A

EXPLANATION OF TERMS

The Office of Personnel Management's *X-118 Qualification Standards Handbook* and their *X-118C Job Qualification System for Trades and Labor Occupations* use a number of terms which have very specific meanings to federal personnel specialists. This appendix lists the key terms, taken from the handbooks.[1]

---

[1] *X-118 Qualification Standards Handbook*, U.S. Office of Personnel Management, Washington, D.C., TS-230, March 1990, pages A-5 through A-7, inclusive; *X-118C Job Qualification System for Trades and Labor Occupations*, U.S. Office of Personnel Management, Washington, D.C., *passim*.

Accredited Education is education above the high school level completed in a U.S. college, university, or other educational institution which has been accredited by one of the accrediting agencies or associations recognized by the Secretary, U.S. Department of Education.

Administrative Series are occupational series which typically follow a two-grade interval pattern and involve the application of a substantial body of knowledge of principles, concepts, and practices applicable to one or more fields of administration or management.

Career-Conditional Appointment is a probationary appointment of one year. If work is satisfactory, the appointment may continue for two additional years for the next two years. Some aspects of civil service protection are withheld, allowing the agency to dismiss the employee. After the third year as a career-conditional appointee, a satisfactory employee is eligible for transition to the competitive service.

Certification is the ranking of all qualified applicants for a vacant position.

Clerical Series are occupational series which follow a one-grade interval pattern and involve structured work in support of office, business, or fiscal operations.

Competitive Appointment is an appointment to a position in the competitive service following open competitive examination or under direct-hire authority. The competitive examination, which is open to all applicants, may consist of a written test, an evaluation of an applicant's education and experience, and/or an evaluation of other attributes necessary for successful performance in the position to be filled.

Competitive Service includes all positions in which appointments are subject to the provisions of chapter 33 of title 5, United States Code. Positions in the executive branch of the federal government are in the competitive service unless they are specifically excluded from it. Positions in the legislative and judicial branches are outside the competitive service unless they are specifically included in it.

Concurrent Experience is experience gained in more than one position, during the same period of time, with either the same employer or with a different employer.

Delegation occurs when job application examinations are done by a federal agency instead of the Office of Personnel Management; full delegation means the agency announces vacancies, recruits applicants and then rates or ranks the applications against the position's qualification standards.

Education above the High School Level is successfully completed progressive study at an accredited business or technical school, junior college, college, or university where the institution normally requires a high school diploma or equivalent for admission.

Fill-in Employment is employment held by persons during the time period after leaving their regular occupation in anticipation of, but before entering, military service.

Foreign Education is education acquired outside the United States, the District of Columbia, the Commonwealth of Puerto Rico, a Trust Territory of the Pacific Islands, or any territory or possession of the U.S.

Full-Time Equivalent (FTE): To federal personnel specialists, a position requiring approximately 40 hours per week of work is one full-time equivalent position. A position requiring 20 hours per week of work is one-half of a FTE position.

Generic Standards are standards prescribed for groups of occupational series which have a common pattern of education and/or experience.

Graduate Education is successfully completed education in a graduate program for which a bachelor's or higher degree is normally required for admission. To be creditable, such education must show evidence of progress through a set curriculum, i.e., it is part of a program leading to a master's or higher degree, and thus does not include post-baccalaureate education consisting of undergraduate and/or continuing education courses which would not lead to an advanced degree.

High School Graduation or Equivalent means the applicant has received a high school diploma, General Education Development (GED) equivalency certificate, or proficiency certificate from a state or territorial-level Board or Department of Education.

Individual Occupational Requirements are requirements (experience, education, etc.) for individual occupational series and are used in conjunction with a generic standard.

Inservice Placement for the purposes of the *X-118 Qualification Standards Handbook* includes promotion, reassignment, change to a lower grade, transfer, reinstatement, reemployment, and restoration, based on an individual's current or former competitive service employment. Inservice placement also includes noncompetitive conversion of excepted appointees whose federal excepted positions are brought into the competitive service under 5 CFR 316.702 and Department of Defense/Nonappropriated Fund (DOD/NAF) employees whose positions are brought into the competitive service. It does not include noncompetitive appointment of non-federal employees whose public or private enterprise positions are brought into the competitive service under 5 CFR 316.701.

Job Family refers to a collection of Wage Grade occupations and job families, based on the nature of the work they do. A job family is a broad grouping of occupations which are related in one or more ways such as: similarity of functions performed, transferability of knowledges and skills from one occupation to another, or similarity of materials or equipment worked on.

Knowledge, Skills and Abilities (KSAs): Knowledge is a body of information applied directly to the performance of a function. Skill is an observable competence to perform a learned psychomotor act. Ability is competence to perform an observable behavior or a behavior that results in an observable product.

Merit Pay is an incentive pay system for GM-13 through GM-15 supervisory personnel; pay increases are based on performance.

Modification of an OPM qualification standard means substitution by an agency or OPM of qualification requirements that differ from those in the published standards. While applicants who qualify under a modified standard may not meet all of the specific requirements described in the published standard, their overall backgrounds show clear evidence of their potential success in the position to be filled. A modified standard may apply to any number of positions within an organization.

Noncompetitive means a promotion, demotion, reassignment, transfer, reinstatement, or appointment in the competitive service that is not made by selection from an open competitive exam or under direct-hire authority.

Normal Line of Promotion is the pattern of upward movement from one grade to another for a position or group of positions in an organization.

Occupation is a subgroup of a Wage Grade job family which includes all jobs at the various skill levels in a particular kind of work. Jobs within an occupation are similar to each other with regard to subject matter and basic knowledge and skill requirements.

Overhire refers to a job which does not have an authorized *position*; a person who is an "overhire" has benefits and rights similar to someone in an authorized position but is also most likely to be the first one to be RIFed when the agency cuts its expenses.

Pay category indicates the type of job and the specific schedule from which the job is paid:

- SES—Senior Executive Service
- GM—General Schedule positions with management responsibilities
- GS—General Schedule positions
- WS—Wage Grade supervisory positions
- WL—Leader jobs in the Wage Grade pay category
- WG—Wage Grade positions, non-supervisory

Position means the officially assigned duties and responsi bilities which make up the work performed by an employee.

Professional series are occupational series which follow a two-grade interval pattern and are identified as "professional" in the series definition. They involve work which is characteristically acquired through education or training equivalent to a bachelor's or higher degree with major study in a specialized field.

Quality Ranking Factors are knowledge, skills and abilities which could be expected to enhance significantly performance in a position, but are not essential for satisfactory performance. Applicants who meet the quality ranking factors may be ranked above those who do not, but no one may be rated ineligible solely for failure to meet a quality ranking factor.

Related Education is education above the high school level which has equipped the applicant with the knowledge, skills, and abilities to perform successfully the duties of the position being filled. Education may relate to the duties of a specific position or to the occupation, but must be appropriate for the position being filled.

Research Positions are positions in professional series which primarily involve scientific inquiry or investigation, or research-type exploratory development of a creative or scientific nature, where the knowledge required to perform the work successfully is acquired typically and primarily through graduate study. The work is such that the academic preparation will equip the applicant to perform fully the professional work of the position after a short orientation period.

Selective Factors are knowledge, skills, abilities, or special qualifications that are in addition to or more specific than the minimum requirements in the qualification standard, but which are determined to be essential to perform the duties and responsibilities of a particular position. Applicants who do not meet a selective factor are ineligible for consideration.

Series or **Occupational Series** means positions similar as to specialized work and qualification requirements. Series are designated by a title and number such as the Accounting Series, GS-510; the Secretary Series, GS-318; the Microbiology Series, GS-403.

Single-Agency Standards are qualification standards, approved by OPM, which are established for positions in a particular agency when the agency's jobs differ substantially from those covered by an OPM standard or for which no government-wide standard is applicable. Single-agency standards supersede the OPM standard for the position they cover.

Specialized Experience is experience which has equipped the applicant with the particular knowledge, skills, and abilities to perform successfully the duties of the position and is typically in or related to the work of the position to be filled.

Status Candidates are job applicants who already work for the federal government. This may be further limited, for example, to "DA Status Candidates." These people already work for the Department of the Army. Applications from people without the mentioned status will not be considered for the vacancy.

Technical series are occupational series which follow a one-grade interval pattern and are associated with and supportive of a professional or administrative **field.**

Veterans Readjustment Appointment is a special appointment for eligible Vietnam era veterans which allows appointment without tests or competition with non-Vietnam veterans, to positions up to GS-11 or WG-11; after two years in such a position, a veteran may be given a competitive appointment; contact a FJIC for further information.

Waiver of an OPM qualification standard involves setting aside requirements in a published standard to place an employee in a particular position usually to avoid some kind of hardship to the employee, such as in cases of reduction-in-force or administrative error on the part of the agency. Extra training and/or skills development may be needed to help the employee adjust to the new position. Waivers are granted by OPM or an agency, as appropriate, on a case-by-case basis, and do not directly affect other positions in the organization.

Work-Study Programs are government or non-government programs that provide supervised work experience related to a student's course of study, which are a part of or a supplement to education. Federal student-trainee programs are examples of such programs.

Appendix B

SELECTED FEDERAL PAY SCHEDULES FOR 1995[1]

General Schedule

GS Grade	Step 1	Step 2	Step 3	Step 4	Step 5	Step 6	Step 7	Step 8	Step 9	Step 10
1	$12,141	$12,546	$12,949	$13,352	$13,757	$13,994	$14,391	$14,793	$14,811	$15,183
2	13,650	13,975	14,428	14,811	14,974	15,414	15,854	16,294	16,734	17,174
3	14,895	15,392	15,889	16,386	16,883	17,380	17,877	18,574	18,871	19,368
4	16,721	17,278	17,835	18,392	18,949	19,506	20,063	20,620	21,177	21,734
5	18,707	19,331	19,955	20,579	21,203	21,827	22,451	23,075	23,699	24,323
6	20,852	21,547	22,242	22,937	23,632	24,327	25,022	25,717	26,412	27,107
7	23,171	23,943	24,715	25,487	26,259	27,031	27,803	28,575	29,347	30,119
8	25,662	26,517	27,372	28,227	29,082	29,937	30,792	31,647	32,502	33,357
9	28,345	29,290	30,235	31,180	32,125	33,070	34,015	34,960	35,905	36,850
10	31,215	32,256	33,297	34,338	35,379	36,420	37,461	38,502	39,543	40,584
11	34,295	35,438	36,581	37,724	38,867	40,010	41,153	42,296	43,439	44,582
12	41,104	42,474	43,844	45,214	46,584	47,954	49,324	50,694	52,064	53,434
13	48,878	50,507	52,136	53,765	55,394	57,023	58,652	60,281	61,910	63,539
14	57,760	59,685	61,610	63,535	65,460	67,385	69,310	71,235	73,160	75,085
15	67,941	70,206	72,471	74,736	77,001	79,266	81,531	83,796	86,061	88,326

[1]The schedules reported in this appendix were established by Executive Order 12826 of December 30, 1992, "Adjustments of Certain Rates of Pay and Allowances," *Federal Register*, Vol 60, No.1, January 3, 1995, pp. 311-314.

Grades 16 through 18 are being converted to SES positions and are unlikely to be used for newly hired employees.

Law Enforcement Schedule

Grade	Step 1	Step 2	Step 3	Step 4	Step 5	Step 6	Step 7	Step 8	Step 9	Step 10
1	$12,379	$12,793	$13,203	$13,614	$14,026	$14,269	$14,673	$15,083	$15,102	$15,487
2	13,917	14,249	14,711	15,102	15,270	15,720	16,169	16,618	17,067	17,517
3	18,226	18,732	19,239	19,745	20,252	20,758	21,265	21,771	22,278	22,784
4	20,456	21,024	21,591	22,159	22,727	23,295	23,863	24,431	24,998	25,566
5	23,522	24,157	24,793	25,428	26,063	26,699	27,334	27,970	28,605	29,241
6	24,802	25,510	26,218	26,927	27,635	28,343	29,051	29,760	30,468	31,176
7	26,775	27,562	28,349	29,137	29,924	30,711	31,498	32,286	33,073	33,860
8	27,910	28,783	29,656	30,528	31,401	32,273	33,146	34,018	34,891	35,764
9	29,864	30,827	31,790	32,753	33,716	34,679	35,642	36,605	37,568	38,531
10	32,888	33,949	35,010	36,070	37,131	38,192	39,253	40,314	41,374	42,435
11	34,968	36,134	37,300	38,465	39,631	40,797	41,963	43,129	44,295	45,460
12	41,910	43,307	44,703	46,100	47,497	48,894	50,290	51,687	53,084	54,480
13	49,837	51,498	53,159	54,819	56,480	58,141	59,802	61,463	63,124	64,785
14	58,892	60,856	62,819	64,783	66,746	68,710	70,673	72,637	74,600	76,564
15	69,273	71,582	73,891	76,200	78,509	80,817	83,126	85,453	87,744	90,053

This table shows pay rates for law enforcement officials in the metro Washington, D.C., Philadelphia, and Chicago areas. Rates are somewhat higher in the New York and San Diego metro areas.

Foreign Service Schedule

Step	Class 1	Class 2	Class 3	Class 4	Class 5	Class 6	Class 7	Class 8	Class 9
1	$67,941	$55,053	$44,609	$36,147	$29,290	$26,184	$23,408	$20,926	$18,707
2	69,979	56,705	45,947	37,231	30,169	26,970	24,110	21,554	19,268
3	72,079	58,406	47,326	38,348	31,074	27,779	24,834	22,200	19,846
4	74,241	60,158	48,745	39,499	32,006	28,612	25,579	22,866	20,442
5	76,468	61,963	50,208	40,684	32,966	29,470	26,346	23,552	21,055
6	78,762	63,822	51,714	41,904	33,955	30,354	27,136	24,259	21,687
7	81,125	65,736	53,265	43,161	34,974	31,265	27,950	24,987	22,337
8	83,559	67,708	54,863	44,456	36,023	32,203	28,789	25,736	23,007
9	86,066	69,739	56,509	45,790	37,104	33,169	29,653	26,508	23,697
10	88,326	71,832	58,205	47,164	38,217	34,164	30,452	27,304	24,408
11	88,326	73,987	59,951	48,579	39,363	35,189	31,458	28,123	25,141
12	88,326	76,206	61,749	50,036	40,544	36,245	32,402	28,966	25,895
13	88,326	78,492	63,602	51,537	41,761	37,332	33,374	29,835	26,672
14	88,326	80,847	65,510	53,083	43,013	38,452	34,375	30,731	27,472

Locality Pay Differentials[2]

Pay Locality	Differential	Pay Locality	Differential
Atlanta MSA	4.66%	Los Angeles	7.39%
Boston	6.97	Miami	5.39
Chicago	6.92	New York	7.30
Cincinnati	5.33	Philadelphia	6.26
Cleveland	4.23	Portland, OR	4.71
Columbus	5.30	Richmond MSA	4.00
Dallas	5.65	Sacramento	5.27
Dayton MSA	5.19	St. Louis MSA	4.28
Denver	5.75	San Diego MSA	6.14
Detroit	6.59	San Francisco	8.14
Houston	8.53	Seattle	5.84
Huntsville MSA	4.39	Washington	5.48
Indianapolis MSA	4.58	Rest of the US	3.74
Kansas City MSA	3.97		

---

[2]Each area below is a Consolidated Metropolitan Statistical Area unless indicated otherwise. MSA refers to a Metropolitan Statistical Area. Both are defined by the Office and Management and Budget (OMB) in *OMB Bulletin Number 94-07*, July 5, 1994.

Appendix C

FEDERAL EMPLOYMENT INFORMATION CENTERS

When writing for job information, be sure to include "Office of Personnel Management" in the mailing address.

Atlanta Region

Office of Personnel Management
75 Spring Street, SW
Atlanta, GA 30303-3109

Alabama
520 Wynn Dr., NW.
Huntsville, AL 35816-3426
(205) 837-0894

Florida
Commodore Bldg., Suite 125
3444 McCrory Pl.
Orlando, FL 32803-3701
(407) 648-6148

Georgia
Richard B. Russell Federal
  Building
Room 940A
75 Spring St., S.W.
Atlanta, GA 30303-3309
(404) 331-4315

Federal Regions

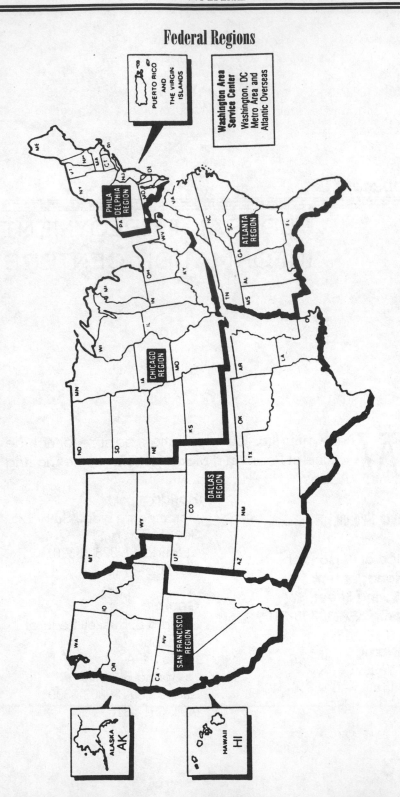

Mississippi
(See Alabama listing)

North Carolina
4407 Bland Rd., Suite 202
Raleigh, NC 27609
(919) 790-2822

South Carolina
(See North Carolina listing)

Tennessee
(See Alabama listing)

Virginia
Federal Bldg., Room 500
200 Granby Street
Norfolk, VA 23510-1886
(804) 441-3355

Chicago Region

**Office of Personnel
  Management
John C. Kluczynski Bldg.
230 South Dearborn Street
Chicago, IL 60604-1687**

Illinois
230 South Dearborn St.
Room 2916
Chicago, IL 60604
(312) 353-6192

(In Madison and St. Clair
Counties [East St. Louis
Area], see St. Louis, MO.
listing)

Indiana
(See Detroit, Michigan)

(In Clark, Dearborn and Floyd
Counties, see Ohio listing)

Iowa
(See Kansas City, MO, listing)
For 24 hour job info: (816)
426-7757. In Scott Co., see Illi-
nois listing. In Pottawattamie
Co., see Kansas listing)

Kansas
(See Kansas City, Missouri)
24 hour job info: (816) 426-7820

Kentucky
(See Ohio listing [except
Henderson Co., see Indiana
listing])

Michigan
477 Michigan Ave.
Room 565
Detroit, MI 48226
(313) 226-6950

Minnesota
Federal Building, Rm 501
1 Federal Drive
Ft. Snelling, MN 55111
(612) 725-3430

Missouri
Federal Building, Rm 134
601 E. 12th St.
Kansas City, MO 64106
(816) 426-5702

(For counties west of and including: Mercer, Grundy, Livingston, Carroll, Saline, Pettis, Benton, Hickory, Dallas, Webster, Douglas and Ozark)

St. Louis
Old Post Office Building
815 Olive St., Room 400
St. Louis, MO 63101
(314) 539-2285
(For all other Missouri counties not listed under Kansas City)

Nebraska
(See Kansas listing.) 24 hour job info: (816) 426-7819

North Dakota
(See Minnesota listing.)

Ohio
200 W. Second St.
Room 506
Dayton, OH 45402
(513) 225-2720
(For counties north of and including Van Wert, Auglaize, Hardin, Marion, Crawford, Richland, Ashland, Wayne, Start, Carroll and Columbiana, see Michigan listing)

South Dakota
(See Minnesota listing.)

West Virginia
(See Ohio listing) 24 hour job info: (513) 225-2866

Wisconsin
(In the counties of Grant, Iowa, Lafayette, Dane, Green, Rock, Jefferson, Walworth, Waukesha, Racine, Kenosha and Milwaukee, see Illinois listing and dial 312-353-6189. For all other Wisconsin counties, see Minnesota listing and dial 612-725-3430)

Dallas Region

Office of Personnel Management
1100 Commerce
Dallas, TX 75250

Arizona
Century Plaza Bldg.
Rm 1415
3225 N. Central Ave.
Phoenix, AZ 85004
(602) 640-4800

Arkansas
(See San Antonio, TX listing.)

Colorado
(mail only)
P.O. Box 25167
Denver, CO 89225

(FJIC is located at 12345 W. Alameda Pkwy, Lakewood, CO) (303) 969-7050
For job information (24 hrs/day) in the following states, dial:

Montana
(See Colorado listing)

Louisiana
1515 Poydras St.
Suite 608
New Orleans, LA 70112
(210) 805-2402

New Mexico
Federal Building
421 Gold Ave., S.W.
Albuquerque, NM 87102
(505) 766-5583
(In Dona Ana and Otero counties in NM and El Paso Co. in TX, dial 505-766-1893)

Oklahoma
(See San Antonio, TX listing)

Texas
Corpus Christi: See San Antonio; (512) 884-8113

Dallas: See San Antonio; (210) 805-2423

Harlingen: See San Antonio; (512) 412-0722

Houston: See San Antonio; (713) 759-0455

San Antonio: Room 305
8610 Broadway,
San Antonio, TX 78217
(210) 805-2406

Utah
(See Colorado listing.)

Wyoming
(See Colorado listing.)

Philadelphia Region

Office of Personnel Management
Federal Building
600 Arch Street
Philadelphia, PA 19106

Connecticut
(See Boston, MA listing)

Delaware
(See Philadelphia, PA listing.)

Maine
(See Boston, MA listing.)

Maryland
(See Philadelphia, PA listing)

Massachusetts
Thos. P. O'Neill Federal Bldg.
10 Causeway St.
Boston, MA 02222-1031
(617) 565-5900

New Hampshire
(See Boston, MA listing)

New Jersey
(For Atlantic, Burlington,
Camden, Cape May,
Cumberland, Gloucester,
Mercer, Monmouth, Ocean
and Salem Counties, see
Philadelphia, PA listing)

(For all other counties, see
New York City, NY listing)

New York
Jacob K. Javits Federal Bldg.
Room 120
26 Federal Plaza
New York, NY 10278
(212) 264-0422

Syracuse
James M. Hanley Federal
   Bldg.
100 S. Clinton St.
Syracuse, NY 13260
(315) 448-0480

Pennsylvania
Federal Bldg., Room 168
P.O. Box 761
Harrisburg, PA 17108
(717) 782-4494

Philadelphia
Wm. J. Green Jr. Federal Bldg.
600 Arch St., Rm 1416
Philadelphia, PA 19106
(215) 597-7440

Pittsburgh
Federal Building, Rm 119
1000 Liberty Avenue
Pittsburgh, PA 15222

Puerto Rico
Federal Bldg.
Room 328
150 Carlos E. Chardon St.
San Juan, PR 00918
(809) 766-5452

Rhode Island
(See Boston, MA listing)

Vermont
(See Boston, MA listing.)

San Francisco Region

Office of Personnel
   Management
211 Main Street
San Francisco, CA 94105

Alaska
222 W. Seventh Ave.
Box 22
Room 156
Anchorage, AK 99513-7572
(907) 271-5821 (From
outside Alaska call (912) 757-
3000)

California
9650 Flair Drive
Suite 100A
El Monte, CA 91731
(818) 575-6510

Sacramento
1029 J St., Room 202
Sacramento, CA 95814
(414) 744-5627

San Diego
Federal Bldg., Room 4260
880 Front St.
San Diego, CA 92101
(818) 575-6510

San Francisco
120 Howard St, Suite B
(mail only)
PO Box 7405
San Francisco, CA 94120.
(415) 744-5627

Hawaii
(And the Pacific Area)
Federal Bldg., Rm 5316
300 Ala Moana Blvd.
Honolulu, HI 96850
(808) 541-2791 (Hawaii)
(912) 757-3000 (Outside
Hawaii)

Idaho
(see Seattle, WA listing.)

Nevada
(For Clark, Lincoln, and Nye
Counties, see Los
Angeles, CA) (For all other
counties see Sacramento, CA
listing.)

Oregon
Federal Bldg., Rm. 376
1220 S.W. Third Ave.
Portland, OR 97204
(503) 326-3141

Washington
Federal Bldg., Rm. 110
915 Second Ave.
Seattle, WA 98174
(206) 220-6400

Washington Area Service Center

**Office of Personnel
   Management
P.O. Box 52
Washington, D.C. 20415
(202) 653-9260
District of Columbia**

(Metropolitan area)
1900 E St., NW
Room 1416
Washington, D.C. 20415
(202) 653-8468

Federal Job Telephone Device For the Deaf (TDD) Numbers

Nationwide TDD Number . . . . (912) 744-2299

Washington D.C. Metropolitan Area . . (202) 606-0591
Southeastern States (AL,FL,GA,MS,NC,SC,TN,
VA) . . . . (919) 790-2739
Northeastern States (CT,DE,ME,MD,MA,NH,NJ,
NY,PA,RI,VT, Puerto Rico, Virgin Islands) . . . . (617)565-8913
North Central States (IL,IN,IA,KS,KY,MI,MN,MO,
NE,ND,OH,SD,WV,WI) . . . . (816) 426-6022
Mountain States (CO,MT,UT,WY) . . . . (303) 969-2739
Southwestern States:
   Arizona . . . . (800) 223-3131
   New Mexico . . . . (505) 766-8662
   Texas (Dallas) . . . . (214) 767-8115
   Rest of Texas . . . . (210) 805-2401
   Louisiana . . . . (504) 589-4636
   Oklahoma/Arkansas . . . . (405) 231-4612
Western States:
   Alaska . . . . (800) 770-8973
   California . . . . (800) 735-2929
   Hawaii . . . . (808) 643-8833
   Idaho . . . . (208) 334-2100
   Nevada . . . . (800) 326-6868
   Oregon . . . . (800) 526-0661
   Washington . . . . (800) 833-6388

Federal Job Opportunities Bulletin Board

(Requires a computer and modem set at least at 2400 baud,
8 data bits, no stop bits, no parity)

Nationwide: . . . . (912) 757-3100
North Central States . . . . (313) 226-4423
Northeastern States . . . . (215) 580-2216
Washington, D.C. area . . . . (202) 606-4800
Western States . . . . (818) 575-6521

(The nationwide board may also be accessed through the Internet (Telnet connections only) at: FJOB.MAIL.OPM.GOV

SELECTED AGENCIES' ADDRESSES

The following addresses do not include positions with Inspector General (IG) offices. Virtually every federal organization has an IG office. These positions are responsible for internal (to the organization) investigations of fraud, waste and mismanagement. Typically, IG positions include auditors, accountants, and management analysts. **The Directory of Federal Jobs and Employers**, by Ronald L. and Caryl Rae Krannich (also from Impact Publications) lists addresses for all federal organizations. Requests for information about IG vacancies should be addressed to Personnel Departments for activities in the **Directory**.

Executive Branch Departments

Agriculture

Forest Service
Dept. of Agriculture
Rosslyn Plaza Bldg E
1621 N. Kent Street
Arlington, VA, 22209

Defense

Defense Investigative
   Service
Resources Directorate
1340 Braddock Place
Alexandria, VA 22314

Air Force Office of Special
   Investigations
Building 626
Bolling Air Force Base
Washington, DC 20332

U.S. Army Criminal
   Investigation Command
5611 Columbia Pike
Falls Church, VA 22041

Naval Criminal Investigative
   Service
Career Service Department
Washington Navy Yard
Bldg 111
901 M Street SE
Washington, D.C. 20388-5380

Health & Human Services

Security Operations Div.
National Institutes of Health
9000 Rockville Pike, Bldg 31
Bethesda, MD 20892

Interior

Division of Law Enforcement
Fish & Wildlife Service
4401 N. Fairfax Drive
Arlington, VA 22203

Bureau of Indian Affairs
Division of Law Enforcement
18th and C Street NW
Washington, DC 20240

National Park Service
Ranger Activities Division
1849 C Street NW
Washington, D.C. 20240

U.S. Park Police
Personnel Office
1100 Ohio Drive SW
Washington, D.C. 20242

Justice

Office of Personnel
Federal Bureau of Prisons
320 First Street NW
Washington, D.C. 20534

Drug Enforcement
  Administration
Personnel Office, Rm 3166
700 Army-Navy Drive
Washington, D.C. 20537

Federal Bureau of
  Investigations
Personnel Resource Office
J. Edgar Hoover FBI Bldg
9th St & Pennsylvania Ave NW
Washington, D.C. 20535

Immigration and
  Naturalization Service
Director of Staffing
1111 Massachusetts Ave, NW
Washington, D.C., 20536

U.S. Marshals Service
Employment Division
Law Enforcement
  Recruiting Br.
600 Army Navy Drive, Rm 890
Arlington, VA 22202

Labor

Occupational Safety and
  Health Administration
Office of Information
200 Constitution Avenue NW
Washington, D.C. 20210

State

Bureau of Diplomatic Security
DS/OAS/PMD, 3d Floor, SA-10
2121 Virginia Avenue, NW
Washington, D.C. 20522-1003

Treasury

Bureau of Alcohol, Tobacco
  and Firearms
650 Massachusetts Avenue
  NW
Washington, D.C. 20226

Internal Revenue Service
National Office Investiga-
tions
  Branch
1111 Constitution Avenue
NW
Washington, D.C. 20224

U.S. Customs Service
Office of Human Resources
Enforcement Division
ATTN: Special Agent
P.O. Box 7108
Washington, D.C. 20044

U.S. Secret Service
Personnel Division
1800 G Street NW
Washington, D.C. 20223

Independent Agencies

Securities & Exchange
  Commission
Classification and Staffing
  Division
450 Fifth Street NW
Washington, D.C.

Environmental Protection
 Agency
Office of Human Resources
 Management
401 M Street SW
Washington, D.C. 20460

Federal Protective Service
Personnel Operations
 Division
General Services
 Administration
18th and F Street NW
Washington, D.C. 20405

U.S. Postal Inspection Service
National Recruitment
 Program Manager
W.F. Bolger Management
 Academy
9600 Newbridge Drive
Potomac, MD 20858

Legislative Branch

Office of Special
 Investigations
General Accounting Office
666 E Street, NW
Washington, D.C. 20004

U.S. Capitol Police HQ
Recruiting Section
119 D Street NW
Washington, D.C. 20510

Judicial Branch

U.S. Supreme Court Police
Supreme Court of the U.S.
Washington, D.C. 20543

GENERAL SCHEDULE
OCCUPATIONS

S ome of the information in this appendix was taken from FOCIS, the Federal Occupational and Career Information System, a computer program prepared by the U.S. Office of Personnel Management and designed to help people select careers in the federal service. A copy of FOCIS may be obtained from the National Technical Information Service. Call (703) 487-4650 for price and ordering information. FOCIS also is available through Impact Publications (see order form at the end of this book). Other information here comes from the *X-118 Qualification Standards Handbook*. An asterisk (*) means that single-agency standards were published for the position in question. If applying for such a position, be sure to ask whether the agency's standards are available.

Boldface job series are law enforcement positions in at least one organization.

GS-000 Miscellaneous Occupations

What do correctional officers, park rangers, firefighters, chaplains and guards have in common? Each of these jobs is unrelated to any other Occupational Group and is, therefore, placed in the Miscellaneous Group.

This group includes all classes of positions which have responsibilities to administer, supervise or perform work not included in any other occupational group either because the duties are unique, complex or come partially under a variety of other groups. The occupations in this group include:

Bond Sales Promotion Representatives (GS-011)
Chaplains (GS-060)
Community Planners (GS-020)
Correctional Institution Administrators (GS-006)
Correctional Officers (GS-007)*
Environmental Protection Assistants (GS-029)
Environmental Protection Specialists (GS-028)
Fingerprint Identifiers (GS-072)*
Firefighters and Fire Inspectors (GS-081)
Foreign Law Specialist (GS-095)*
General Student Trainee (GS-099)
Nuclear Materials Courier (GS-084)*
Outdoor Recreation Planners (GS-023)
Park Rangers and Park Managers (GS-025)
Police Officers (GS-083)
Safety and Occupational Health Specialists (GS-018)
Safety Technicians (GS-019)
Security Guards (GS-085)
Security Specialists (GS-080)
Sports Specialists (GS-030)
U.S. Marshals (GS-082)*

GS-100 Social Science, Psychology and Welfare

Social sciences and social services deal with cultures and people. Social sciences deal with psychology, economics, history, sociology and anthropology. Social services deal with social work, recreational activities and the administration of public welfare and insurance programs.

The positions in this group carry responsibilities for advising, administering, supervising or performing research or other professional and scientific work, or subordinate technical work or related clerical work. The occupations in this group include:

Anthropologists (GS-190)
Archaeologists (GS-193)
Civil Rights Analyst (GS-160)
Economists (GS-110)
Foreign Agricultural Affairs
    Specialists (GS-135)
Food Assistance Program
    Specialists (GS-120)*
Foreign Affairs Specialists
    (GS-130)
Geographers (GS-150)
Historians (GS-170)
Intelligence Aides and
    Clerks (GS-134)
Intelligence Specialists
    (GS-132)
International Cooperation
    Specialists (GS-136)*
Manpower Development
    Specialists (GS-142)

Psychologists (GS-180)
Psychology Aides and
    Technicians (GS-181)
Recreation Specialists
    (GS-188)
Social Insurance
    Administrators (GS-105)*
Social Science Aides
    and Technicians (GS-102)
Social Scientists (GS-101)
Social Science Student
    Trainee (GS-199)
Social Service Aides and
    Assistants (GS-186)
Social Service
    Representatives (GS-187)
Social Workers (GS-185)
Unemployment Insurance
    Specialists (GS-106)*

GS-200 Personnel Management and Industrial Relations

The Federal Government operates on people power. This resource, called personnel, fluctuates. Each agency has a personnel office staffed with personnel specialists who hire, fire, train employees, administer a variety of personnel programs and overall, perform work involving the various aspects of human resources management and industrial relations. The occupations in this group include:

Apprenticeship and Training
  Representatives (GS-243)*
Contractor Industrial Relations
  Specialists (GS-246)
Employee Development
  Specialists (GS-235)
Employee Relations
  Specialists (GS-230)
Equal Employment
  Opportunity Specialists
  (GS-260)
Labor Management Relations
  Examiners (GS-244)*
Labor Relations Specialists
  (GS-233)
Mediators (GS-241)*
Military Personnel Clerks
  and Technicians (GS-204)

Military Personnel
  Management Specialists
  (GS-205)
Personnel Clerks and
  Assistants (GS-203)
Personnel Management
  Specialists (GS-201)
Personnel Management
  Student Trainee (GS-299)
Personnel Staffing
  Specialists (GS-212)
Position Classification
  Specialists (GS-221)
Salary and Wage
  Administrators (GS-223)
Wage and Hour Compliance
  Specialists (GS-249)*

GS-300 Administrative, Clerical, and Office Services

This group includes all classes of positions which have responsibilities for administering, supervising or performing work involving management analysis; stenography, typing and secretarial work; mail and file tasks; the operation of computers, office machines and communications equipment; the technical phases of photographic and art processes; and, overall, performing general clerical and administrative work. The occupations in this group include:

Administrative Officers (GS-341)

Administration and Office Support Student Trainee (GS-399)

Clerk-Stenographers and Reporters (GS-312)

Clerk-Typists (GS-322)

Closed Microphone Reporters (GS-319)

Coding Clerks (GS-357)

Communications Clerks (GS-394)

Communications Managers (GS-391)

Communications Relay Operators (GS-390)

Communications Specialists (GS-393)

Computer Clerks and Assistants (GS-335)

Computer Operators (GS-332)

Computer Specialists (GS-334)

Correspondence Clerks (GS-309)

Data Transcribers (GS-356)

Equal Opportunity Compliance Specialists (GS-360)

Equipment Operators (GS-350)

General Communications Specialists (GS-392)

Logistics Management Specialists (GS-346)

Mail and File Clerks (GS-305)

Management Analysts (GS-343)

Management Clerks and Assistants (GS-344)

Miscellaneous Clerks and Assistants (GS-303)

Program Analysts (GS-345)

Secretaries (GS-318)

Support Services Administrators (GS-342)

A shortage exists in the Federal government of qualified secretaries, clerks, typists and stenographers.

GS-400 Biological Sciences

Biologists and related scientists use their knowledge to detect and to control pests and diseases and to develop new strains and promote growth of useful organisms. In this group, the positions carry responsibilities for advising, administering, supervising or performing research or other professional and scientific work or subordinate technical work in any of the science fields concerned with living organisms; the soil and its properties and distribution; and the management, conservation and use of these resources. The occupations in this group include:

Agricultural Management Specialists (GS-475)*
Agricultural Extension Agent (GS-406)
Agronomists (GS-471)
Animal Scientists (GS-487)
Biological Science Student Trainee (GS-499)
Biological Technicians (GS-404)
Botanists (GS-430)
Ecologists (GS-408)
Entomologists (GS-414)
Fish and Wildlife Administrators (GS-480)
Fish and Wildlife Refuge Managers (GS-485)
Fishery Biologists (GS-482)*
Foresters (GS-460)
Forestry Technicians (GS-462)
General Biological Scientists (GS-401)
Geneticists (GS-440)
Home Economists (GS-493)

Horticulturists (GS-437)
Irrigation System Operators (GS-459)*
Microbiologists (GS-403)
Pharmacologists (GS-405)
Physiologists (GS-413)
Plant Pathologists (GS-434)
Plant Physiologists (GS-435)
Plant Protection and Quarantine Officers (GS-436)*
Plant Protection Technicians (GS-421)*
Range Conservationists (GS-454)
Range Technicians (GS-455)
Soil Conservationists (GS-457)
Soil Conservation Technicians (GS-458)
Soil Scientists (GS-470)
Wildlife Biologists (GS-486)
Wildlife Refuge Manager (GS-485)*
Zoologists (GS-410)

GS-500 Accounting and Budget

Money and accountability go hand-in-hand. Taxpayers and program managers require efficient use and management of Federal dollars; so the Federal Government employs financial experts in virtually all of its agencies. The people in these positions advise, administer, supervise or perform professional, technical or related clerical work of an accounting, budget administration or financial management nature. The occupations in this group include:

Accountants (GS-510)
Accounting Technicians
  (GS-525)
Auditors (GS-511)
Budget Analysts (GS-560)
Cash Processors (GS-530)
Financial Administrators
  (GS-501)
**Financial Institution
  Examiners (GS-570)**
Financial Managers
  (GS-505)
Financial Management
  Student Trainee (GS-599)

Insurance Accounts
  Specialists (GS-593)
**Internal Revenue Agents
  (GS-512)***
Military Pay Specialists
  (GS-545)
Payroll Clerks and
  Technicians (GS-544)
Tax Examiners (GS-592)*
Tax Technicians (GS-526)*
Voucher Examiners (GS-540)

GS-600 Medical, Hospital, Dental and Public Health

The Nation's health is overseen, maintained and improved upon by the many doctors, dentists, therapists, allied health specialists, nurses, health administrators and health-care support staff employed by the Federal Government. The people in these positions advise, administer, supervise or perform research or other professional and scientific work, subordinate technical work or related clerical work in one of the many branches of medicine, surgery, dentistry and related patient-care fields. The occupations in this group include:

Autopsy Assistants (GS-625)
Consumer Safety Officers
  (GS-696)*
Corrective Therapists (GS-635)
Dental Assistants (GS-681)

Dental Hygienists (GS-682)
Dental Laboratory Aides and
  Technicians (GS-683)
Dentists (GS-680)

Diagnostic Radiologic Technologists (GS-647)

Dietitians and Nutritionists (GS-630)

Doctors (GS-602)

Educational Therapists (GS-639)

Environmental Health Technicians (GS-698)

General Health Scientists (GS-601)

Health Aides and Technicians (GS-640)

Health System Administrators (GS-670)

Health System Specialists (GS-671)

Hospital Housekeepers (GS-673)

Industrial Hygienists (GS-690)

Manual Arts Therapists (GS-637)

Medical Clerks (GS-679)

Medical and Health Student Trainee (GS-699)

Medical Machine Technicians (GS-649)

Medical Records Librarians (GS-669)

Medical Records Technicians (GS-675)

Medical Supply Aides and Technicians (GS-622)

Medical Technologists (GS-644)

Medical Technical Assistant (GS-650)*

Nuclear Medicine Technicians (GS-642)

Nurses (GS-610)

Nursing Assistants (GS-621)

Occupational Therapists (GS-631)

Optometrists (GS-662)

Orthotists/Prosthetists (GS 667)

Pathology Technicians (GS-646)

Pharmacists (GS-660)

Pharmacy Technicians (GS-661)

Physical Therapists (GS-633)

Physicians Assistants (GS-603)

Podiatrists (GS-668)

Practical Nurses (GS-620)

Prosthetic Representatives (GS-672)

Public Health Advisors and Analysts (GS-685)*

Recreation and Creative Arts Therapists (GS-638)

Rehabilitation Therapy Assistants (GS-636)

Respiratory Therapists (GS-651)

Restoration Technicians (GS-664)*

Speech Pathologists and Audiologists (GS-665)

Therapeutic Radiologic Technologists (GS-648)

There are many opportunities in the public sector for doctors and dentists, audiologists, dietitians, medical records administrators, Orthotists/Prosthetists, pharmacists, speech pathologists, physical therapists and nurses across the U.S.

GS-700 Veterinary Medical Science

Livestock diseases, meat and poultry processing operations, laboratory research, and animal health and welfare are areas of concern to the Federal Government. The positions in this group carry responsibilities for advising and consulting, administering, managing, supervising or performing research or other professional and scientific work in the various branches of veterinary medical science. The occupations in this group include:

> Animal Health Technicians (GS-704)
> Veterinarians (GS-701)
> Veterinary Student Trainee (GS-799)

GS-800 Engineering and Architecture

Engineers and architects perform professional and scientific work in the design and construction of projects such as buildings, systems, equipment, materials and methods. They also review applications, designs, and plans for structures and systems.

The positions in this group require a knowledge of the science or the art, or both, in order to transform and make useful materials, natural resources and power. The occupations in this group include:

Aerospace Engineers (GS-861)
Agricultural Engineers (GS-890)

Architects (GS-808)
Biomedical Engineers (GS-858)
Ceramic Engineers (GS-892)

Chemical Engineers (GS-893)

Civil Engineers (GS-810)

Computer Engineers (GS-854)

Construction Analysts (GS-828)

Construction Control (GS-809)

Drafting Engineers (GS-818)

Electrical Engineers (GS-850)

Electronics Engineers (GS-855)

Electronics Technicians (GS-856)

Engineering and Architecture Student Trainee (GS-899)

Engineering Technicians (GS-802)

Engineers (GS-801)

Environmental Engineers (GS-819)

Fire Prevention Engineers (GS-804)

General Engineer (GS-801)

Industrial Engineering Technicians (GS-895)

Industrial Engineers (GS-896)

Industrial Engineer Technicians (GS-895)

Landscape Architect (GS-807)

Materials Engineers (GS-806)

Mechanical Engineers (GS-830)

Mining Engineers (GS-880)

Naval Architects (GS-871)

Nuclear Engineers (GS-840)

Petroleum Engineers (GS-881)

Safety Engineers (GS-803)

Ship Surveyors (GS-873)

Surveying Technicians (GS-817)

There are numerous opportunities for engineers in all specialties with the Federal Government across the United States.

GS-900 Legal and Kindred

Courtroom drama, lawyers, judges and examiners with their magnifying glasses are all part of the legal arena. Any agency is likely to employ attorneys either in its legal department or in its Office of the General Counsel.

This group includes all classes of positions which carry responsibilities for advising, administering, supervising or performing professional legal work in preparation for the trial and argument of cases; presiding at formal hearings; administering laws entrusted to an agency or department; providing authoritative or advisory legal opinions or decisions; preparing a variety of legal documents; and performing quasi-legal work. The occupations in this group include:

Administrative Law Judges (GS-935)

Attorneys (GS-905)

Civil Service Retirement Claim Examiners (GS-997)*

Claims Clerks (GS-998)

Clerk of Court (GS-945)

Contract Representatives (GS-962)

Estate Tax Examiners (GS-920)

General Claims Examiners (GS-990)

Hearings and Appeals Specialists (GS-930)

Land Law Examiners (GS-965)*

Law Clerks (GS-904)

Legal Clerks and Technicians (GS-986)

Legal Instruments Examiners (GS-963)

Legal Occupations Student Trainee (GS-999)

Loss and Damage Claims Examiners (GS-992)

Paralegal Specialists (GS-950)

Social Insurance Claims Examiners (GS-993)*

Unemployment Compensation Claims Examiners (GS-994)*

Veterans Claims Examiners (GS-996)*

Visa and Passport Examiners (GS-967)*

Worker's Compensation Claims Examiners (GS-991)*

GS-1000 Public Information and Arts

The world of public information, music, theater, language, museums, photography, writing and illustrating is a world away from the typical Federal job. The Federal Government maintains and operates theaters, audio-visual production facilities, museums, and public information programs. The positions in this group require writing, editing and foreign languages; the ability to evaluate and to interpret informational and cultural materials; the ability to apply technical or aesthetic principles in combination with manual skills and dexterity; and possess clerical skills. The occupations in this group include:

Arts Specialists (GS-1056)
Audio-Visual Production
  Specialists (GS-1071)
Editorial Assistants
  (GS-1087)
Exhibits Specialists
  (GS-1010)
General Arts and
  Information Specialist
  (GS-1001)
Illustrators (GS-1020)
Information and Arts
  Student Trainee (GS-1099)
Interior Designer (GS-1008)
Language Clerk (GS-1046)
Language Specialists
  (GS-1040)

Museum Curators (GS-1015)
Museum Specialists and
  Technicians (GS-1016)
Music Specialist (GS-1051)
Office Drafting Specialist
  (GS-1021)
Photographers (GS-1060)
Public Affairs Specialists
  (GS-1035)
Technical Writers and Editors
  (GS-1083)
Theater Specialist (GS-1054)
Visual Information
  Specialists (GS-1084)
Writers and Editors (GS-1082)

GS-1100 Business and Industry

The business world and the Federal world have many similar needs. Both deal daily with contracts, property, purchasing, production and finances. Industrial production methods and processes, industrial and commercial contracts, and the examination and appraisal of merchandise or property are some of the business and trade activities of the Government. The positions in this group carry responsibilities for advising, administering, supervising or performing work pertaining to and requiring a knowledge of business and industry rules, regulations and practices. The occupations in this group include:

Agricultural Marketing
  Specialists (GS-1146)*

Agricultural Market
  Reporters (GS-1147)*

Agricultural Program
Specialists (GS-1145)*
Appraisers and Assessors
(GS-1171)
Building Manager
(GS-1176)*
Business and Industry
Specialists (GS-1101)
Business and Industry
Student Trainee (GS-1199)
Commissary Store Managers
(GS-1144)
Contract Specialists
(GS-1102)
Crop Insurance
Administrators (GS-1161)*
Crop Insurance Underwriter
(GS-1162)*
Financial Analysts (GS-1160)
Housing Managers
(GS-1173)
Industrial Property
Managers (GS-1103)

Industrial Specialists
(GS-1150)
Insurance Examiner
(GS-1163)
Internal Revenue Officers
(GS-1169)*
Loan Specialists (GS-1165)
Procurement Clerks and
Assistants (GS-1106)
Production Controllers
(GS-1152)
Property Disposal Clerks
and Technicians (GS-1107)
Property Disposal Specialists
(GS-1104)
Public Utilities Specialists
(GS-1130)
Purchasing Specialists
(GS-1105)
Realtors (GS-1170)
Trade Specialists (GS-1140)

GS-1200 Copyright, Patent and Trademark

When does an invention become an invention? Who keeps track of all the designs, applications and details for copyright and patent approvals? The U.S. Patent Office within the Department of Commerce handles inquiries, applications and recordkeeping functions in this arena.

This group includes positions having the responsibilities for advising, administering, supervising, or performing professional scientific, technical and legal work related to copyright cataloguing and registration; patent classification and issuance; and trademark registration. The occupations in this group include:

Copyright and Patent
  Student Trainee (GS-1299)
Copyright Specialist
  (GS-1210)
Copyright Technician
  (GS-1211)
Design Patent Examiner
  (GS-1226)*
Patent Administrator
  (GS-1220)

Patent Advisor (GS-1221)
Patent Attorneys (GS-1222)*
Patent Classifier (GS-1223)*
Patent Examiners
  (GS-1224)*
Patent Interference
  Examiner (GS-1225)*
Patent Technician
  (GS 1202)

GS-1300 Physical Sciences

The physical world can be divided into three sections for scientific study: earth, water and space. The people employed in this group administer, supervise, advise or perform research, professional and scientific work or subordinate technical work in any of the science fields concerned with matter, energy, physical space, time, nature of physical measurement and the physical environment, and the fundamental structural particles. Occupations in this group include:

Astronomers and Space
  Scientists (GS-1330)
Cartographers (GS-1370)
Cartographic Technicians
  (GS-1371)
Chemists (GS-1320)
Food Technologists (GS-1382)
General Physical Scientists
  (GS-1301)
Geodesists (GS-1372)
Geologists (GS-1350)
Geophysicists (GS-1313)
Health Physicists (GS-1306)
Hydrologic Technicians
  (GS-1316)
Hydrologists (GS-1315)

Land Surveyors
  (GS-1373)
Metallurgists (GS-1321)
Meteorological
  Technicians
  (GS-1341)
Meteorologists
  (GS-1340)
Navigational Information
  Specialists (GS-1361)
Oceanographers
  (GS-1360)
Physical Science
  Student Trainee
  (GS-1399)

Physical Science   Physicists (GS-1310)
Technicians (GS-1311)

GS-1400 Library and Archives

The library may outwardly seem a sedentary place. Behind the scenes, people busily collect, organize, preserve and retrieve information. The staff at any Federal library helps to keep the Government's records up-to-date. The people employed in this group work in the various phases of library and archival science and have responsibilities to supervise, administer, advise and perform professional and scientific work or subordinate technical work. The occupations in this group include:

Archivists (GS-1420)*   Library and Archives Student
Archives Technicians   Trainee (GS-1499)
  (GS-1421)   Library Technicians (GS-1411)
Librarians (GS-1410)   Technical Information Services
                                   Specialists (GS-1412)

GS-1500 Mathematics and Statistics

People apply mathematical, statistical and financial principles to every facet of daily life and business. This group includes all classes of positions carrying responsibilities for advising, administering, supervising and performing research or other professional and scientific work or related clerical work using mathematical principles, methods, procedures or relationships. The occupations in this group include:

Actuaries (GS-1510)   Mathematical Statisticians
Computer Science Specialists   (GS-1529)
  (GS-1550)   Mathematicians (GS-1520)
Cryptographer (GS-1540)   Mathematics and Statistics
Cryptanalysts (GS-1541)   Student Trainee (GS-1599)

Operations Research   Statisticians (GS-1530)
Analysts (GS-1515)

GS-1600 Equipment, Facilities and Service

Federally owned property may be located anywhere in the United States or around the world. A property site may include facilities, services and, often, buildings to be managed. The positions in this group require technical or managerial skills and abilities, plus a practical knowledge of trades, crafts or manual-labor operations.

The people employed in this group must carry out the responsibilities for advising, managing, or providing instructions and information to others in such functions. The occupations in this group include:

Cemetery Superintendents   General Facilities and
  (GS-1630)*   Equipment Specialists
Equipment and Facilities   (GS-1601)
  Student Trainee (GS-1699)   Laundry and Dry Cleaning
Equipment Specialists   Plant Managers (GS-1658)
  (GS-1670)   Printing Specialists (GS-1654)
Facility Managers (GS-1640)   Stewards (GS-1667)

GS-1700 Education

The Federal Government continually trains new employees and supervisors and provides continuing, refresher and retraining courses to its employees. The curricula and opportunities are diverse. This group includes positions which involve administering, managing, supervising, performing or supporting education or training. The occupations in this group include:

Educational Program Specialists   Education and Training
  (GS-1720)*   Specialists (GS-1701)

Education and Training
Technicians (GS-1702)
Education and Vocational
Training Specialists
(GS-1710)
Education Researcher
(GS-1730)*
Education Specialist
(GS-1740)
Education Student Trainee
(GS-1799)
Elementary Teachers
(GS-1724)

Public Health Educators
(GS-1725)
School Administrators
(GS-1722)
Secondary Teachers
(GS-1726)
Special Ed. Teachers
(GS-1728)
Training Instructors
(GS-1712)
Vocational Rehabilitation
Specialists (GS-1715)

GS-1800 Investigation

Sniffing out criminals, following clues, gathering and presenting evidence, observing people and merchandise entering the United States, investigating prospective Federal employees, and working undercover are all duties within the Investigation Group.

The Federal Government hires people for investigation, inspection and enforcement work to uphold and safeguard the laws, the people and the property of the United States. The occupations in this group include:

Agricultural Commodity
Warehouse Examiners
(GS-1850)*
Air Safety Investigators
(GS-1815)*
**Alcohol, Tobacco, and
Firearms Inspectors
(GS-1854)***
Aviation Safety Inspectors
(GS-1825)*
**Border Patrol Agents
(GS-1896)***

Compliance Inspection and
Support Specialists
(GS-1802)
Consumer Safety Inspectors
(GS-1862)*
**Criminal Investigators
(GS-1811)**
Customs Aides (GS-1897)
Customs Entry and
Liquidation
Specialists (GS-1894)*

Customs Inspectors
(GS-1890)*
Customs Patrol Officers
(GS-1884)*
Customs Warehouse Officer
(GS-1895)*
Food Inspectors (GS-1863)*
Game Law Enforcement
Agents (GS-1812)
General Inspection,
Investigation and
Compliance Specialists
(GS-1801)

General Investigators
(GS-1810)
Immigration Inspectors
(GS-1816)*
Import Specialists (GS-1889)
Investigation Student
Trainee (GS-1899)
Mine Safety and Health
Inspectors (GS-1822)*
Public Health Quarantine
Inspector (GS-1864)*
Securities Compliance
Examiners (GS-1831)

GS-1900 Quality Assurance, Inspection and Grading

In this age of technological sophistication and excellence, government operations demand quality products. Quality products depend on quality materials, facilities and processes. The Federal Government performs inspections and commodities grading to bring products up to standard levels.

The people employed in this group advise, supervise or perform administrative or technical work related to quality assurance, inspection or commodities grading. The occupations in this group include:

Agricultural Commodity Aides
(GS-1981)
Agricultural Commodity
Graders (GS-1980)

Assurance Officer
(GS-1910)
Quality Inspection Student
Trainee (GS-1999)

GS-2000 Supply

It takes many different types of items to operate the Federal government. Each item is identified, selected and acquired; then it is counted, catalogued and distributed prior to being stored, inventoried or used. The positions in this group require knowledge of one or more elements of supply systems, and/or supply methods, policies or procedures.

Work performed within this group concerns the provision and control of supplies, equipment, material, property (except real estate) and other services to components of the Federal government, or industrial or other concerns under contract to the government or receiving supplies from the government. The occupations in this group include:

Distribution Facility and Storage Management Specialists (GS-2030)
Inventory Management Specialists (GS-2010)
Packaging Specialists (GS-2032)
Sales Stores Clerks (GS-2091)
Supply Catalogers (GS-2050)

Supply Clerks and Technicians (GS-2005)
Supply Program Managers (GS-2003)
Supply Specialists (GS-2001)
Supply Student Trainee (GS-2099)

GS-2100 Transportation

The federal government requires many transportation services and regulates a variety of transportation activities. This group includes positions having responsibilities for advising, administering, supervising or performing clerical, administrative or technical work involved in providing transportation service to the Government, regulating Government transportation activities, or managing Government-funded transportation programs including research and development projects. The occupations in this group include:

Aircraft Operators (GS-2181)

Air Navigation Specialist (GS-2183)

Aircrew Technician (GS-2185)

Air Traffic Assistants (GS-2154)

Air Traffic Controllers (GS-2152)

Cargo Schedulers (GS-2144)

Dispatchers (GS-2151)

Freight Rate Specialists (GS-2131)

Highway Safety Specialists (GS-2125)*

Marine Cargo Specialists (GS-2161)

Motor Carrier Safety Specialists (GS-2123)*

Railroad Safety Inspectors and Specialists (GS-2121)*

Shipment Clerks and Assistants (GS-2134)

Traffic Management Specialists (GS-2130)

Transportation Clerks and Assistants (GS-2102)

Transportation Industry Analysts (GS-2110)

Transportation Loss Damage Claims Examiners (GS-2135)

Transportation Operators (GS-2150)

Transportation Specialists (GS-2101)

Transportation Student Trainee (GS-2199)

Travel Assistants (GS-2132)

SAMPLE JOB ANNOUNCEMENTS

GAME WARDEN, GS-1802-07, GS-1812-07

VACANCY ANNOUNCEMENT

Provost Marshal Office, Operations Division
Fort Belvoir, VA

Announcement Number: FB-08-48-95-AE
Issue Date: 09-05-95
Closing Date:09-19-95

Salary: $24,441 to 31,770[1]

---

[1]The salary includes a Geographic Adjustment.

WHO MAY APPLY: All qualified candidates. All status candidates who wish to be considered under both merit promotion and competitive procedures must submit two (2) complete applications. When only one (1) application is received, it will be considered under the merit promotion announcement only.

DUTIES: Serves as a Game Warden on Fort Belvoir with responsibility for protecting fish and wildlife resources and controlling human activities to ensure appropriate management of these resources while providing optimum community benefits. Patrols Fort Belvoir ranges including housing areas, which includes over 8,000 square acres. Enforces installation, state and federal fish and wildlife laws, regulations and policies. During hunting season, controls and monitors the hunters on the range. Inspects permits, licenses, clothing worn, and weapons for compliance with the law. Ensures that hunters keep within defined areas during hunting season, and ensures that all hunters comply with state, federal and installation laws. Searches for lost persons on the range. Investigates all reports of animal bites. Informs the public of the danger of rabies from wild animals; speaks formally and informally to groups at Fort Belvoir on this topic. Monitors the deer population on the ranges and coordinates deer herd relocation. While patrolling the range, report any type of incident which requires attention, such as brush fires, abandoned vehicles, or any other type of unusual activity. Conducts investigations into violations of Federal fish and wildlife laws which involve the full range of difficult and complex law enforcement activities to include surveillance, participation in raids, interviewing witnesses, interrogating suspects, searching for and processing physical evidence, seizing contraband, securing crime scenes, securing and serving search warrants, making apprehensions, inspecting records and documents, developing information for orderly presentations to the U.S. Magistrate, U.S. Attorney, or other legal officers, testifying in court, preparing detailed written reports, and conducting undercover operations for short periods of time.

QUALIFICATIONS REQUIRED: One year of specialized experience equivalent to the GS-5. Specialized experience is experience that has equipped the applicant with the particular knowledge, skill and abilities to perform successfully the duties of the position and that is typically in or related to the work of the position to be filled.

WORKING CONDITIONS: Work includes both office and outdoor settings. There is regular and recurring exposure to moderate risks and discomforts such as adverse weather conditions, high/low temperatures, duty/noisy environment, etc. Assignments include surveillance work in various vehicles and on foot.

CONDITIONS OF EMPLOYMENT: Work is performed day and night, during weekends and irregular hours. Satisfactory completion of medical examination required. As a precondition and continuation of employment, any and all incumbents of this position must agree to submit to urinalysis on a recurring basis. Possess valid driver's license to operate a 4-wheel drive vehicle on secondary roads and in forested areas. Required to bear and maintain proficiency in the use of hand and shoulder-fired firearms, and incapacitating devices and materials.

HOW TO APPLY: You *must* apply with a *typed* OF 612 (Optional Application for Federal Employment). No computer generated version of the OF 612 (that is not a exact duplicate) will be accepted.

To claim 5-point veterans' preference, attach a copy of your DD 214, Certificate of Release or Discharge from

Active Duty, or other proof of eligibility. To claim 10-point veterans' preference, attach an SF 15, Application for Veterans' Preference, plus the proof required by that form.

In addition, applicants are required to submit the following documents:

- SF 50, Notification of Personnel Action showing status.
- Supervisory evaluation of related factors.
- Background Survey Questionnaire (Optional).
- Supplemental Information Sheet.
- E.O 12721 candidates must submit verification of eligibility.
- NAF employees must submit appropriate forms documenting one year of permanent DOD NAF service.

FOR FURTHER INFORMATION CALL Jay Allen (703)...

SUPERVISORY EVALUATION OF JOB/RELATED FACTORS

SUBMISSION OF THE SUPERVISORY EVALUATION OF JOB/ RELATED FACTORS IS MANDATORY FOR CURRENT FEDERAL APPLICANTS APPLYING FOR PROMOTION OPPORTUNITY.

PLEASE CIRCLE THE APPROPRIATE NUMBER TO INDICATE LEVEL OF PERFORMANCE.

4=Superior   3=Highly Successful   2=Fully Successful
1=Marginal   0=Unable to appraise

EVALUATION FACTORS	LEVEL OF PERFORMANCE

FACTOR 1: Knowledge of fish and wildlife laws and regulations (Federal, State, County and Fort Belvoir Installation)   4   3   2   1   0

FACTOR 2: Ability to conduct criminal investigation of fish and wildlife law violations.   4   3   2   1   0

FACTOR 3: Ability to communicate in writing   4   3   2   1   0

FACTOR 4: Ability to communicate orally and testify in court.   4   3   2   1   0

SUPERVISOR'S SIGNATURE   DATE

The following job announcement is an example of a position requiring status in the federal service.

UNITED STATES DEPARTMENT OF INTERIOR
FISH AND WILDLIFE SERVICE
VACANCY ANNOUNCEMENT

This Is a Drug-testing Designated Position. Applicant(s) tentatively selected for this position will be required prior to appointment to submit to urinalysis to screen for illegal drug use. As a condition of continued employment in this position, incumbent(s) will be subject to random testing for illegal drug use.

POSITION: Refuge Law Enforcement Officer

ANNOUNCEMENT NUMBER: FWS4-95-73, GS-1802-05/06

SALARY RANGE: $19407—$28121

OPENING DATE: August 28, 1995
FULL PERFORMANCE LEVEL: GS-1802-06

CLOSING DATE: September 18, 1995
AREA OF CONSIDERATION: Department-wide

LOCATION: Arm Loxahatchee National Wildlife Refuge, Boynton Beach, Florida

CONTACT TELEPHONE NUMBER: (404) 679-4014 (404) 679-4052

ADDRESS OF PERSONNEL OFFICE: Fish And Wildlife Service

U.S. Fish and Wildlife Service
Personnel Division Suite 370
1875 Century Boulevard
Atlanta, GA 30345

Incumbent must be able to operate a government-owned or leased motor vehicle. A valid state driver's license is required. Selectee may be assigned classified work or work in a classified area which will require background investigation.

APPLICATIONS UNDER THIS ANNOUNCEMENT WILL BE ACCEPTED ONLY FROM QUALIFIED STATUS CANDIDATES OR FROM QUALIFIED CANDIDATES ELIGIBLE UNDER SPECIAL APPOINTING AUTHORITY. ELIGIBILITY FOR APPOINTMENT MUST BE INDICATED ON THE 171.

The incumbent will be required to obtain and wear an official U.S. Fish and Wildlife Service uniform. The incumbent will be required to occupy Government-furnished quarters on Federal premises.

The person selected for this position will be required to submit an SF-78, Certificate of Medical Examination, if the form is not already on file. The incumbent will be required to accept and exercise law enforcement authority.

QUALIFICATION REQUIREMENTS FOR THE GS-5 LEVEL: Candidates must have 1 year of specialized experience equivalent to the GS-4 level; OR 4 years above high school.

QUALIFICATION REQUIREMENTS FOR THE GS-6 LEVEL: Candidates must have 1 year of specialized experience equivalent to the GS-5 level.

SPECIALIZED EXPERIENCE: Experience which is directly related to law enforcement and which has equipped the candidate with the particular knowledge, skills, and abilities to successfully perform the duties of a Refuge Law Enforcement Officer.

CONDITIONS OF EMPLOYMENT:

1. Incumbent is required to work weekends and holidays on a variable tour of duty.

2. *Notice to All Male Applicants*: All male applicants born after December 31, 1959, must sign a Pre-Appointment Certification Statement for selective Service Registration. All candidates will be considered without regard to race, creed, color, sex, age, national origin, political affiliation, religion, handicap or any other non-merit factor. Applicants must meet all eligibility requirements for this position, including time-in-grade requirements, within 30 days of the closing date.

STATEMENT OF DUTIES: Incumbent serves as the Refuge Law Enforcement Officer at ARM Loxahatchee National Wildlife Refuge in Boynton Beach, Florida. Incumbent enforces all applicable state and federal fish and wildlife laws and refuge regulations; conducts both short-term and long-term investigations involving fish and wildlife violations, breaking and entering, theft of government property, controlled substance, etc.; maintains cooperative relationships and liaison with appropriate service, local, state, and federal law enforcement personnel; prepares cases for presentation before U.S. Magistrate-Judge or State or local courts.

HOW TO APPLY: The following forms should be submitted.

Applications lacking these forms will be disqualified or will not be given full consideration for this position.

1. A complete up-to-date Standard Form 171 (Application for Federal Employment), resume, or Optional Form 612 (Application for Federal Employment).

2. A copy of your most recent SF-50 (Notification of Personnel Action) that confirms your career or career-conditional status.

3. A narrative statement addressing each ranking factor.

4. Supervisory Appraisal for Merit Promotion, R4-208 (4-90). This office is equipped with a Telephone Device for the Deaf (TDD). Hearing impaired individuals with TDD equipment may contact us at 404/679-4051. In accordance with 39 U.S.C. Section 415, applications will not be accepted in a postage paid agency envelope (Penalty Mail). Applications become the property of the Service and will not be returned for referred or other vacancies. NOTE: If you choose to submit a resume or an alternative format, you must include your name, telephone number, home address, social security number, date of birth, employers address, description of related work/employment, beginning and ending dates of employment (month/year), hours worked per week, citizenship and any other information specified in this announcement.

KNOWLEDGES, ABILITIES, SKILLS AND OTHER CHARAC-
TERISTICS (KASOCS):

1. Knowledge of law enforcement methods and techniques.

2. Ability to work effectively with local, State, and Federal law enforcement personnel.

3. Ability to plan and organize day-to-day law enforcement activities.

4. Ability to communicate orally.

5. Ability to communicate in writing.

6. Ability to interpret observations, draw sound conclu-
   sions, and act accordingly in dealing with a variety of
   law enforcement situations.

DEPARTMENT'S APPLICANT BACKGROUND SURVEY,
DI-1935: The completion of DI-1935 is strictly voluntary and
is used for statistics purposes only by the Office for Human
Resources. All DI-1935s become the property of the Office
for Human Resources and are not shared in the evaluation
process or with the selecting official.

All applicants tentatively selected for this position will be
required to submit to urinalysis to screen for illegal drug
use prior to appointment.

HATCH ACT PROVISIONS: The Hatch Act Reform Amend-
ments of 1993 (Public Law 103-94) prohibit individuals from
requesting, making, transmitting, accepting, or considering
political recommendations (as defined in 5 U.S.C. 3303) in
effecting personnel actions.

The following vacancy announcement is typical of the entry-level "police" or "guard" positions offered throughout the federal government.

National Gallery of Art
Vacancy Announcement

ANNOUNCEMENT NO.	95-AOP
ISSUE DATE	2-3-95
CLOSING DATE	OPEN UNTIL FILLED

POSITION	POTENTIAL	SALARY RANGE
SECURITY GUARD GS-085-4 (Multiple Vacancies)	------	$18,949-$23,962 P/A

LOCATION	AREA OF CONSIDERATION
Office of Protection Services Administrator's Staff	Federal Status Candidates and * VRA eligibles

* Veterans Readjustment Appointment (VRA) eligibles are Vietnam-era (8/5/64 - 5/7/75) and post-Vietnam-era veterans who served more than 180 days active duty and have other than a dishonorable discharge.

DUTIES:·
The position is located in the Office of Protection Services and the incumbent is responsible for protecting the valuable and irreplaceable works of art; checking articles and parcels in and out of the Checkrooms; protecting the Gallery's buildings, persons, and property therein; maintaining order and decorum; and enforcing rules and regulations established by proper authorities.

QUALIFICATIONS:
Candidates must meet the *Qualifications Standards Handbook* for GS-085-4. This requires six months of general experience and six months of specialized experience or 2 years of full-time education above the high school level. General experience is administrative, technical, clerical or military office work. Specialized experience is work with Federal, state, municipal, local, or private protection organizations that involved the protection of property against such hazards as fire, theft, damage, accident, or trespass; or maintaining order and protecting life.

THE SELECTED CANDIDATE MUST HAVE A SATISFACTORY SUITABILITY DETERMINATION BASED ON A BACKGROUND INVESTIGATION BEFORE BEING HIRED FOR THIS POSITION

CANDIDATES MUST SUBMIT A COPY OF THEIR DD-214 AND/OR SF-50 WITH THEIR APPLICATION.

HOW TO APPLY:

1. Submit either OF 612 "Optional Application for Federal Employment" or resume to:
   Personnel Office
   National Gallery of Art
   Washington, D. C. 20565
   202/842-6282

24-HOUR DIAL-A-JOB
202/842-6298
TDD 202/789-3021

NGA Form 266: revised 8/93

POSITION QUALIFICATION STANDARDS

There are six GS families or groups of job series; each has been given a general set of qualification standards. Excerpts from the *X-118 Qualification Standards Handbook*, showing minimum requirements for three of the families, with law enforcement positions, are provided here. Further information may be obtained from the *Handbook*, Part IV.

Administrative, Management and Specialist Positions

The positions in this group have two intervals between grades. Someone promoted from a grade 7 position, for example, is promoted not to grade 8 but to grade 9. As might be expected from the group name, education requirements are more stringent and after the lowest grade (5), general experience is not important. At the journeyman level (above grade 11), only specialized experience in the job series qualifies one for a position. Typically, jobs in this family will also have fairly specific KSAOs or additional qualification requirements in job announcements. Normally this makes entry from outside the federal government quite difficult for most of the jobs in the family.

MINIMUM QUALIFICATION REQUIREMENTS FOR TWO-GRADE INTERVAL ADMINISTRATIVE, MANAGEMENT, AND SPECIALIST POSITIONS

This qualification standard covers positions in the General Schedule which involve the performance of two-grade interval administrative, management, and specialist work. A list of the occupational series covered by this qualification standard is provided below. This standard may also be used for other two-grade interval positions for which the education and experience pattern is determined to be appropriate. While some of the occupational series covered by this standard include both one- and two-grade interval work, the qualification requirements described in this standard apply only to those positions which follow a two-grade interval pattern.

This standard contains common patterns of undergraduate and graduate education, general and specialized experience, and other information to be used in making qualifications determinations. Some occupations covered by this standard contain education or experience requirements which are more specific than the requirements described in the generic standard. These requirements are provided in attachments to the basic standard. Such occupations are noted below with an asterisk. For a description of the work performed in occupations covered by this standard, refer to the series definitions in the *Handbook of Occupational Groups and Series* and-or to individual positions' classification standards.

GS-011	Bond Sales Promotion*	GS-360	Equal Opportunity Compliance
GS-018	Safety and Occupations Health Management*	GS-362	Electric Accounting Machine Project Planning
GS-023	Outdoor Recreation Planning*	GS-391	Telecommunications*
GS-028	Environmental Protection Specialist	GS-501	Financial Administration and Program
GS-030	Sports Specialist*	GS-505	Financial Management
GS-062	Clothing Design*	GS-560	Budget Analysis
GS-080	Security Administration	GS-570	Financial Institution Examining*
GS-105	Social Insurance Administration	GS-669	Medical Records Administration*
GS-106	Unemployment Insurance*	GS-670	Health System Administration*
GS-120	Food Assistance Program Specialist	GS-671	Health System Specialist*
GS-132	Intelligence	GS-673	Hospital Housekeeping Management*
GS-142	Manpower Development	GS-685	Public Health Program Specialist*
GS-160	Civil Rights Analysis	GS-828	Construction Analyst*
GS-188	Recreation Specialist*	GS-920	Estate Tax Examining
GS-201	Personnel Management	GS-930	Hearings and Appeals
GS-205	Military Personnel Management	GS-950	Paralegal Specialist
GS-212	Personnel Staffing	GS-958	Pension Law Specialist*
GS-221	Position Classification	GS-962	Contact Representative
GS-222	Occupational Analysis	GS-965	Land Law Examining*
GS-223	Salary and Wage Administration	GS-990	General Claims Examining
GS-230	Employee Relations	GS-991	Workers' Compensation Claims Examining
GS-233	Labor Relations	GS-993	Social Insurance Claims Examining
GS-235	Employee Development	GS-996	Veterans Claims Examining
GS-244	Labor Management Relations Examining*	GS-1001	General Arts and Information
GS-246	Contractor Industrial Relations	GS-1008	Interior Design*
GS-260	Equal Employment Opportunity	GS-1010	Exhibits Specialist*
GS-270	Federal Retirement Benefits	GS-1020	Illustrating*
GS-301	Miscellaneous Administration and Program	GS-1035	Public Affairs
GS-334	Computer Specialist*	GS-1040	Language Specialist*
GS-340	Program Management	GS-1051	Music Specialist*
GS-341	Administrative Officer	GS-1054	Theater Specialist*
GS-343	Management and Program Analysis	GS-1056	Art Specialist*
GS-346	Logistics Management		

GS-1071 Audio-Visual Production*
GS-1082 Writing and Editing
GS-1083 Technical Writing and Editing*
GS-1084 Visual Information*
GS-1101 General Business and Industry*
GS-1103 Industrial Property Management*
GS-1104 Property Disposal
GS-1130 Public Utilities Specialist
GS-1140 Trade Specialist*
GS-1144 Commissary Store Management*
GS-1150 Industrial Specialist*
GS-1160 Financial Analysis*
GS-1163 Insurance Examining*
GS-1165 Loan Specialist*
GS-1170 Realty
GS-1171 Appraising and Assessing
GS-1173 Housing Management
GS-1176 Building Management
GS-1361 Navigational Information*
GS-1397 Document Analysis*
GS-1421 Archives Specialist
GS-1630 Cemetery Administration
GS-1640 Facility Management*
GS-1654 Printing Management*
GS-1670 Equipment Specialist*
GS-1702 Education and Training Technician
GS-1712 Training Instruction*
GS-1715 Vocational Rehabilitation*
GS-1801 General Inspection, Investigation, and
         Compliance*

GS-1810 General Investigating
GS-1811 Criminal Investigating*
GS-1812 Game Law Enforcement
GS-1816 Immigration Inspection
GS-1831 Securities Compliance Examining*
GS-1854 Alcohol, Tobacco and Firearms
         Inspection*
GS-1864 Public Health Quarantine
         Inspection*
GS-1890 Customs Inspection*
GS-1910 Quality Assurance*
GS-2001 General Supply
GS-2003 Supply Program Management
GS-2010 Inventory Management
GS-2030 Distribution Facilities and Storage
         Management
GS-2032 Packaging
GS-2050 Supply Cataloging
GS-2101 Transportation Specialist*
GS-2110 Transportation Industry Analysis*
GS-2123 Motor Carrier Safety*
GS-2125 Highway Safety*
GS-2130 Traffic Management*
GS-2150 Transportation Operations*
GS-2161 Marine Cargo*

The requirements of this standard have been approved for the following occupations for use within the Veterans Health Administration of the Department of Veterans Affairs under the provisions of section 7402, title 38, U.S.C.: GS-301, Miscellaneous Administration and Program, except for GS-301, Rehabilitation Medicine Coordinator positions; GS-340, Program Management; GS-669, Medical Records Administration; GS-670, Health System Administration; GS-671, Health System Specialist; GS-672, Prosthetic Representative,; GS-673, Hospital Housekeeping Management; GS-1020, Illustrating; GS-1101, General Business and Industry; and GS-1715, Vocational Rehabilitation.

EDUCATION AND EXPERIENCE REQUIRE-
MENTS

GS-5 and above: The following table shows the
amounts of education and experience required for
grades GS-5/15 for positions covered by this
standard. Applicants who meet experience requirements for a higher grade also meet the
experience requirements for positions at lower
grades in the same occupation. Possession of an
advance degree, e.g., Ph.D., without having
earned the lesser degree, e.g., M.A., qualifies an
applicant for both the appropriate higher and
lower grades.

Grade	Education	OR	Experience	
			General	Specialized
GS-5	4-year course of study above high school leading to a bachelor's degree		3 years, 1 year of which was at least equivalent to GS-4	None
GS-7	1 full academic year of graduate level education or law school or superior academic achievement		None	1 year at least equivalent To GS-5
GS-9	2 full academic years of progressively higher level graduate education or master's or equivalent graduate degree or LL.B. or J.D.		None	1 year at least equivalent to GS-7
GS-11	3 full academic years of progressively higher level graduate education or Ph.D or equivalent doctoral degree		None	1 year at least equivalent to GS-9
GS-12 & above	None		None	1 year at least equivalent next lower grade level

Equivalent combinations of education and experience are qualifying for all grade levels for which
both education and experience are acceptable.

Undergraduate Education

Successful completion of a full 4-year course of
study *in any field* leading to a bachelor's degree,
in an accredited college or university, meets the
requirements at the GS-5 level for all positions,
except for those covered by separate attachments
to this standard. Applicants for the latter positions
must, in general, (1) have specific course work
that meets the requirements for a major in a
particular field(s), or (2) have at least 24 semester
hours of course work in the field(s) identified in
the attachment covering the occupation. Course
work in fields closely related to those specified
may be accepted if it clearly provides applicants
with the background of knowledge and skills
necessary for successful job performance. One
year of full-time undergraduate study is defined as

30 semester hours or 45 quarter hours, and is
equivalent to 9 months of general experience.

The superior academic achievement provision
for entry at GS-7 is applicable to all occupations covered by this standard.

Graduate Education

Education at the graduate level (including law
school education) in an accredited college or
university in the amounts shown in the table
meets the requirements for positions at GS-7
through GS-11. Such education must demonstrate the knowledge, skills, and abilities necessary to do the work.

A year of full-time graduate education is considered to be the number of credit hours which
the school attended has determined to represent 1 year of full-time study. If that information cannot be obtained from the school, 18
semester hours should be considered as satisfy-
ing the 1 year of full-time study requirement.
Part-time graduate education is creditable in
accordance with its relationship to a year of
full-time study at the school attended.

For certain positions covered by this standard,
the work may be recognized as sufficiently
technical or specialized, and the working level
such that graduate study alone may not provide
the knowledge and skills needed to perform the
work. In such cases, agencies may use selective factors to screen out applicants without
actual work experience.

General Experience

Three years of progressively responsible experience which demonstrates the ability to:

1. Analyze problems to identify significant factors, gather pertinent data, and
   recognize solutions;

2. Plan and organize work; and

3. Communicate effectively orally and in
   writing.

Such experience may have been gained in
administrative, professional, technical, investigative, or other responsible work. Experience
in substantive and relevant secretarial, clerical,
or other responsible work may be qualifying as

long as it has provided evidence of the knowledge, skills, and abilities (KSA's) necessary to perform the duties of the position to be filled. Experience of a general clerical nature (typing, filing, routine procedural processing, maintaining records, or other nonspecialized tasks) is not creditable. Trades or crafts experience appropriate to the position to be filled may also be creditable for some positions. Specialized experience may be substituted for general experience.

For some occupations, applicants must have had work experience which demonstrated KSA's in addition to those identified above. Positions with more specific general experience requirements than those described here are shown in the attachment covering the occupation(s). (Also, see the information below on use of selective factors.)

Specialized Experience

Experience which has equipped the applicant with the particular knowledge, skills, and abilities to perform successfully the duties of the position and which is typically in or related to the work of the position to be filled. To be creditable, specialized experience must have been at least equivalent to the next lower grade level in the normal line of progression for the occupation in the organization.

Combining Education and Experience

Combinations of successfully completed education and experience may be used to meet total qualification requirements, and may be computed by first determining the applicant's total qualifying experience as a percentage of the experience required for the grade level; then determining the applicant's education as a percentage of the experience required for the grade level; and then adding the two percentages. The total percentages must equal at least 100 percent to qualify an applicant for that grade level. Only graduate education in excess of the amount required for the next lower grade level may be used to qualify applicants for positions at grades GS-9 and GS-11. (When crediting education which requires specific course work, prorate the number of hours of related courses required as a proportion of the total education to be used.)

The following are examples of how education and experience may be combined. They are examples only, and are not all-inclusive.

- The position to be filled is a Loan Specialist, GS-1165-5. An applicant has 2 years of general experience and 45 semester hours of college, which includes 9 semester hours in related course work as described in the attachment. The applicant meets 67 percent of the required experience and 38 percent of the required education. Therefore, the applicant exceeds 100 percent of the total requirement and is qualified for the position.

- The position to be filled is a Management Analyst, GS-343-9. An applicant has 6 months of specialized experience equivalent to GS-7 and 1 year or graduate level education. The applicant meets 50 percent of the required experience but none of the required education, since he or she does not have any graduate study beyond that which is required for GS-7. Therefore, the applicant meets only 50 percent of the total requirement and is not qualified for the position. (The applicant's first year of graduate study is not qualifying for GS-9.)

- The position to be filled is a Music Specialist, GS-1051-11. An applicant has 9 months of specialized experience equivalent to GS-9 and 2 ½ years of creditable graduate level education in music. The applicant meets 75 percent of the required experience and 50 percent of the required education, i.e., the applicant has ½ year of graduate study beyond that required for GS-9. Therefore, the applicant exceeds the total requirement and is qualified for the position. (The applicant's first 2 years of graduate study are not qualifying for GS-11.)

OTHER QUALIFICATION PROVISIONS

Applicants for positions in some occupations must meet certification or licensing requirements in addition to meeting the education/experience requirements described above. Applicants can qualify on the basis of licensure, certification, or registration in lieu of education or experience in some other occupations. Such provisions are noted in the attachment covering the occupation.

USE OF SELECTIVE FACTORS

Agencies may identify some positions covered

by this standard that require knowledge, skills, and abilities or other qualifications, such as certification or licensure, that are in addition to or more specific than the minimum requirements described in this standard. The need for these special requirements can be met through the use of selective factors in both the competitive and inservice recruitment processes. Selective factors may be used for all of the occupations covered by this standard. They must be job related, essential for the successful performance of the position, and represent KSA's or other qualifications which could not be reasonably acquired on the job during the period of training customary for the position being filled.

WRITTEN TEST REQUIREMENTS

For information on the occupational series and positions covered by this standard which require written tests, refer to the *Test Requirements in Qualification Standards* section (Part IV) of this Handbook.

Student Trainee Positions

STUDENT TRAINING QUALIFICATION STANDARD FOR COMPETITIVE SERVICE POSITIONS

This standard describes the qualification requirements for student trainees under career-conditional or career appointments in the competitive service. Eligibility and selection requirements for prospective competitive service student trainees are described in FPM Chapter 332, Appendix G. Student trainee positions in the excepted service are covered by the Multiseries Student Trainee Qualification Standard for Schedule B Positions. This standard is not applicable to students who are temporarily employed during the summer vacations and who have not been appointed to a student trainee program in the competitive service as described above.

Students may be appointed to any position which leads to qualification in a two-grade interval professional, administrative, or technical occupational series. Following is a list of the occupational series covered by this standard.

GS-099 General Student Trainee Series	GS-1399 Physical Science Student Trainee Series
GS-199 General Science Student Trainee Series	GS-1499 Library and Archives Student Trainee Series
GS-299 Personnel Management Student Trainee Series	GS-1599 Mathematics and Statistics Student Trainee Series
GS-399 Administration and Office Support Student Trainee Series	GS-1699 Equipment and Facilities Student Trainee Series
GS-499 Biological Science Student Trainee Series	GS-1799 Education Student Trainee Series
GS-599 Financial Management Student Trainee Series	GS-1899 Investigation Student Trainee Series
GS-699 Medical and Health Student Trainee Series	GS-1999 Quality Inspection Student Trainee Series
GS-799 Veterinary Student Trainee Series	GS-2099 Supply Student Trainee Series
GS-899 Engineering and Architecture Student Trainee Series	GS-2199 Transportation Student Trainee Series
GS 999 Legal Occupations Student Trainee Series	GS-1099 Information and Arts Student Trainee Series
GS-1299 Copyright and Patent Student Trainee Series	GS-1199 Business and Industry Student Trainee Series

This standard has been approved by the Administrator of Veterans Affairs for use within the Department of Medicine and Surgery of the Veterans Administration under the provisions of section 4105, title 38, U.S.C.

Student trainees qualify as described below.

GRADE	LEVEL OF EDUCATION
GS-2	High school diploma or equivalent
GS-3	Completion of 1 academic year post-high school
GS-4	Completion of 2 academic years of post-high school or associate's degree

The required education must lead to a bachelor's degree with specialization in or directly related to the field in which they will receive training on the job. The degree of specialization in this field must satisfy on graduation the specific educational requirements in the qualification standard for the corresponding two-grade interval positions.

PROMOTION REQUIREMENTS

Student trainees may be promoted to higher-graded trainee positions based on completion of portions of the education and student trainee work experience.

To GS-3: Completion of one full semester, or the equivalent, of post-high school study and one period of student trainee work experience.

To GS-4: (a) Completion of 1 academic year of study and two periods of student trainee work experience; or (b) completion of 1½ academic

years of study and one period of student trainee work experience.

To GS-5: (a) Completion of 3 academic years of study and one period of GS-4 student trainee work experience; or (b) completion of 2 ½ academic years of study and 6 months (at least 960 hours) of GS-4 student trainee work experience.

Upon completion of all the requirements for a bachelor's degree in an appropriate field, student trainees may be reassigned or promoted in the appropriate target series to GS-5 or GS-7, if they meet the qualification requirements of the target occupation, including minimum education requirements, if any.

EXPLANATION OF TERMS

An academic year of undergraduate education is defined as 30 semester hours, 45 quarter hours, or the equivalent in an accredited college or university.

For purposes of this standard, a period of student trainee work experience is the equivalent of 2 months (320 hours) of full-time work experience.

WRITTEN TESTS

No written test is required for these positions.

Clerical and Administrative Support Positions

The standards listed on the next four pages are general standards for a group of similar jobs which have a single grade interval. That is, people in these jobs normally advance one grade level when they get promoted. Notice how general experience (in all the job families in this appendix) decline in importance while specialized experience increases, as grade levels increase. Also, above grade 5, education does not generally substitute for experience.

These are general standards; more specific requirements are in the X-118 Qualification Standards Handbook.

MINIMUM QUALIFICATION REQUIREMENTS FOR ONE-GRADE INTERVAL CLERICAL AND ADMINISTRATIVE SUPPORT POSITIONS

This qualification standard covers positions in the General Schedule which involve the performance of one-grade interval clerical and administrative support work. A list of the occupational series covered by this standard is provided below. This standard may also be used for other one-grade interval positions for which the education and experience pattern is determined to be appropriate. While some of the occupational series

covered by this standard include both one- and two-grade interval work, the qualification requirements described in this standard apply only to those positions which follow a one-grade interval pattern. For a description of the work in these occupations, refer to the series definitions in the *Handbook of Occupational Groups and Series* and/or to individual position classification standards.

GS-029 Environmental Protection Assistant
GS-072 Fingerprint Identification
GS-086 Security Clerical and Assistance
GS-134 Intelligence Aid and Clerk
GS-203 Personnel Clerical and Assistance
GS-204 Military Personnel Clerical and Technician
GS-302 Messenger[1]
GS-303 Miscellaneous Clerk and Assistant
GS-304 Information Receptionist
GS-305 Mail and File
GS-309 Correspondence Clerk
GS-312 Clerk-Stenographer and Reporter
GS-318 Secretary
GS-319 Closed Microphone Reporting
GS-322 Clerk-Typist
GS-326 Office Automation Clerical and Assistance
GS-332 Computer Operation
GS-335 Computer Clerk and Assistant
GS-344 Management Clerical and Assistance
GS-350 Equipment Operator
GS-351 Printing Clerical
GS-356 Data Transcriber
GS-357 Coding
GS-359 Electric Accounting Machine Operation
GS-361 Equal Opportunity Assistance
GS-382 Telephone Operating
GS-390 Telecommunications Processing
GS-392 General Telecommunications
GS-394 Communications Clerical
GS-503 Financial Clerical and Assistance
GS-525 Accounting Technician
GS-530 Cash Processing
GS-540 Voucher Examining

GS-544 Civilian Pay
GS-545 Military Pay
GS-561 Budget Clerical and Assistance
GS-592 Tax Examining
GS-593 Insurance Accounts
GS-675 Medical Records Technician
GS-679 Medical Clerk
GS-962 Contact Representative
GS-963 Legal Instruments Examining
GS-986 Legal Clerical and Assistance
GS-990 General Claims Examining
GS-998 Claims Clerical
GS-1001 General Arts and Information
GS-1046 Language Clerical
GS-1087 Editorial Assistance
GS-1101 General Business and Industry
GS-1105 Purchasing
GS-1106 Procurement Clerical and Assistance
GS-1107 Property Disposal Clerical and Technician
GS-1152 Production Control
GS-1411 Library Technician[2]
GS-1421 Archives Technician
GS-1531 Statistical Assistant
GS-1702 Education and Training Technician
GS-1802 Compliance Inspection and Support
GS-1897 Customs Aid
GS-2005 Supply Clerical and Technician
GS-2091 Sales Store Clerical
GS-2102 Transportation Rate and Tariff Examining
GS-2131 Freight Rate
GS-2132 Travel
GS-2133 Passenger Rate

[1]Under 5 U.S.C. 3310, appointment to Messenger positions is restricted to persons entitled to veteran preference as long as such persons are available.

[2]These qualification requirements have been approved for use within the Veterans Health Administration of the Department of Veterans Affairs under the provisions of section 7402, title 38, U.S.C.

GS-2134 Shipment Clerical and Assistance
GS-2135 Transportation Loss and Damage
Claims Examining

EDUCATION AND EXPERIENCE REQUIREMENTS

GS-1/6 and above: The following table shows the amounts of general and/or specialized experience and education that meet the requirements for each grade.

Grade/Positions	Experience		OR	Education
	General	Specialized		
GS-1 All positions	None	None		None
GS-2 All positions	3 months	None		High school graduation or equivalent
GS-3 Clerk-Steno				High school graduation or equivalent
All other positions	6 months	None		1 year above high school
GS-4 All positions	1 year	None		2 years above high school
GS-5 Clerk-Steno	2 years	None		4 years above high school (There is no educational substitution for Reporting Stenographer, Shorthand Reporter, or Closed Microphone Reporter positions.)
All other positions	None	1 year at least equivalent to GS-4		
GS-6 and above All positions	None	1 year at least equivalent to next lower grade level		Generally, not applicable

Equivalent combinations of education and experience are qualifying for all grade levels and positions for which both education and experience are acceptable.

General Experience—(All positions except Reporting Stenographer, Shorthand Reporter, and Closed Microphone Reporter): Progressively responsible clerical, office, or other work which indicates ability to acquire the particular knowledge, skills, and abilities (KSA's) to perform successfully the duties of that position and which is typically in or related to the position to be filled. To be creditable, specialized experience must have been at least equivalent to the next lower grade level.

Specialized Experience—(All positions except Reporting Stenographer, Shorthand Reporter, and Closed Microphone Reporter): Experience which has equipped the applicant with the particular knowledge, skills, and abilities (KSA's) to perform successfully the duties of that position and which is typically in or related to the position to be filled. To be creditable, specialized experience must have been at least equivalent to the next lower grade level.

GS-2151 Dispatching

Experience for Reporting Stenographer, Shorthand Reporter, and Closed Microphone Reporter—One year of experience at least equivalent to the next lower grade level using the skills and equipment appropriate to the position to be filled is required for all positions. Following is a description of qualifying experience for these positions.

Reporting Stenographer, GS-5: Experience as a clerk-stenographer, secretary, reporting stenographer, or in another position which included application of stenography and typing skills as a significant part of the work. Reporting Stenographer, Shorthand Reporter, and Closed Microphone Reporter, GS-6: Experience as a reporting stenographer, hearing reporter, or in another position in which the primary duty was to make and transcribe manual or machine-written shorthand records of hearings, interviews, or similar proceedings. Shorthand Reporter and Closed Microphone Reporter, GS-7 and above: Experience as a court reporter, or hearing reporter, or in another position in which the primary duty was to make verbatim records of proceedings.

Education

High school graduation or the equivalent is creditable at the GS-2 level for the occupations listed, except Clerk-Stenographer, where it is creditable at the GS-3 entry level.

Successfully completed education above the high school level in any field for which high school graduation or the equivalent is the normal prerequisite is creditable at grades GS-3 through GS-5 for all positions except Reporting Stenographer, GS-5. This education must have been obtained in an accredited business, secretarial or technical school, junior college, college or university. One full year of full-time academic study is 30 semester hours, 45 quarter hours, or the equivalent of college or at least 20 hours of classroom instruction per week for approximately 36 weeks in a business, secretarial, or technical school.

As a general rule, education is not creditable

above GS-5 for most positions covered by this standard; however, graduate education may be credited in those few instances where the graduate education is directly related to the work of the position.

Intensive Short-Term Training—Completion of an intensive, specialized course of study of less than 1 year (such as for computer operator) may meet in full the experience requirements for GS-3. Courses of this type normally require completion of up to 40 hours per week of instruction rather than the usual 20 hours per week and are usually of *at least* 3 months duration. Such courses may have been obtained through a variety of programs such as those offered by business or technical schools, and through military training programs. To be creditable, such a course must have been designed specifically as career preparation for work of the position being filled and must have provided the applicant with the necessary knowledge, skills and abilities to do the work.

Combining Education and Experience

Equivalent combinations of successfully completed post-high school education and experience may be used to meet total experience requirements at grades GS-5 and below, except for Reporting Stenographer, GS-5.

For GS-3 and GS-4 level positions, determine the applicant's total qualifying experience as a percentage of the experience required for the grade level; then determine the applicant's education as a percentage of the education required for the grade level; then add the two percentages. The total percentage must equal at least 100 percent to qualify an applicant for the grade level.

For all GS-5 level positions (except Clerk-Stenographer, which does not require specialized experience), only education in excess of the first 60 semester hours (i.e., beyond the second year) is creditable toward meeting the specialized experience requirement. One full academic year of study (30 semester hours) *beyond the second year* is equivalent to 6 months of specialized experience.

The following are examples of how education and experience may be combined. They are examples only, and are not all inclusive:

- The position to be filled is a Payroll Clerk,

GS-4. An applicant has 8 months of qualifying experience and 20 semester hours of college. The applicant meets 67 percent of the required experience and 33 percent of the required education. The applicant meets 100 percent of the total requirements and is qualified for the position.

- The position to be filled is a Clerk-Typist, GS-4. The applicant has 4 months of qualifying experience and 1 year of business school. The applicant meets 33 percent of the required experience and 50 percent of the required education. The applicant meets 83 percent of the total requirements and is not qualified for the position.

- The position to be filled is a Clerk-Stenographer, GS-5. An applicant has 1 year of qualifying experience and 90 semester hours of college. The applicant meets 50 percent of the required experience and 75 percent of the required education. The applicant exceeds 100 percent of the total requirements and is qualified for the position.

- The position to be filled is a Personnel Clerk, GS-5. The applicant has 9 months of specialized experience and 75 semester hours of college (15 semester hours beyond the second year and the equivalent of 3 months of specialized experience). The applicant meets 75 percent of the required experience and 25 percent of the required education. The applicant meets 100 percent of the requirement of 1 year of specialized experience and is qualified for the position.

USE OF SELECTIVE FACTORS

Agencies may identify some positions in an occupation, especially at the higher grade levels, that require KSA's that are in addition to or more specific than the minimum requirements described in this standard. The need for these special requirements can be met through the use of selective factors in both the competitive and inservice recruitment processes. Selective factors must be job related, essential for the successful performance of the position, and represent KSA's which could not be reasonably acquired on the job during the period of training customary for the position being filled.

WRITTEN TEST REQUIREMENTS

For information on the occupational series and positions covered by this standard which require written tests, refer to the *Test Requirements in Qualification Standards* section (Part IV) of this Handbook.

PROFICIENCY REQUIREMENTS

Clerk-Typist, Office Automation Clerk/Assistant, Clerk-Stenographer, Data Transcriber, and Positions with Parenthetical Titles of (Typing), (Office Automation), (Stenography), or (Data Transcription)

In addition to meeting experience or education requirements, applicants for these positions must show possession of the following skills, as appropriate. Applicants may meet these requirements by passing the appropriate performance test, presenting a certificate of proficiency from a school or other organization authorized to issue such certificates by the Office of Personnel Management local office, or by self-certifying their proficiency. Performance test results and certificates of proficiency are acceptable for 3 years. Agencies may verify proficiency skills of self-certified applicants by administering the appropriate performance test.

Clerk-Typist, GS-2/3, Office Automation Clerk/Assistant (any grade), (typing) (any grade), and (Office Automation) (any grade):
   40 words per minute typing speed

Data transcriber, GS-2/4, and (Data Transcription) (any grade):
   skill in operating an alphanumeric data transcribing machine,
   or 20 words per minute typing speed for GS-2 transcription duties,
   or 25 words per minute typing speed for GS-3 and GS-4 transcription duties

Clerk-Stenographer, GS-3/4:
   40 words per minute typing speed *and*
   80 words per minute dictation speed

Clerk-Stenographer, GS-5:
   40 words per minute typing speed *and*
   120 words per minute dictation speed

(Stenography) (any grade):
   40 words per minute typing speed *and either*
   80 words per minute dictation speed for GS-3

and GS-4 stenographic duties or
120 words per minute dictation speed for GS-5 stenographic duties

NOTE: The level of proficiency for stenographic and data transcribing duties required by positions with parenthetical titles is based on the grade level of those duties and not necessarily on the overall grade of the position. For example, a position classified as Secretary (Stenography), GS-318-5, may require either 80 or 120 words per minute dictation speed depending upon the level of difficulty of the stenographic duties. Or, a position classified as a Payroll Clerk (Data Transcription), GS-544-4, may require either 20 or 25 word per minute typing speed depending upon the level of difficulty of the transcribing duties. Therefore, before filling positions of this type, first determine the grade level of the duties which require the additional skill, and then determine the skill level required.

Reporting Stenographer, Shorthand Reporter, and Closed Microphone Reporter

In addition to meeting the experience requirements, applicants for these positions must show possession of the following skills with equipment appropriate to the specific position.
   Reporting Stenographer, GS-5/6: 120 words per minute dictation speed
   Shorthand Reporter and Closed Microphone Reporter, GS-6: 160 words per minute dictation speed
   Shorthand Reporter and Closed Microphone Reporter, GS-7 and above: 175 words per minute dictation speed

Applicants must also be able to produce accurate typewritten transcripts of recorded proceedings.

Applicants for competitive appointment and inservice applicants for initial assignment to these three positions at all grade levels must demonstrate the specific skill and level of proficiency required by the position to be filled. Also, inservice applicants for promotion of positions which have a higher proficiency requirement than the position previously held must demonstrate the higher level of proficiency. Applicants may demonstrate the proficiency by either passing a dictation test at the required speed or presenting a certificate of proficiency showing speed and accuracy equivalent to those used in the Office of Personnel Management performance tests for these positions. The certificate must show that the candidate demonstrated the required proficiency, i.e., dictation speed and accuracy, to a teacher or stenography, shorthand reporting, or closed microphone reporting, within the past year. Applicants for these positions may not self-certify dictation proficiency.

SAMPLE APPLICATION CHECKLIST

I.   LIST ASSETS

A. Identify, in general terms, your:

1. Educational background.

2. Previous paid and unpaid work/efforts.

B. Identify, in general terms, where you want to work.

C. What federal organizations appeal to you?

II. Identify jobs AND grades for which you are eligible by:

A. Using FOCIS

B. Get advice from OPM or state employment counselors.

C. Scan appendices in this book (job series and, for GS jobs, the general qualification standards).

III. Focus on the requirements for target jobs:

A. Identify any required exams.

    1. Call nearest OPM for test dates and sites.

    2. Check libraries for hints, sample questions, or copies of old exams.

B. Review X-118/X118C standards and agency-made standards.

    1. Determine whether your assets qualify you for the target job.

    2. Does the target series/grade appeal to you?

    3. Are you almost qualified for other series or grades?

IV. Get current job announcements from:

A. OPM's FEICs or the *Career America Connection*.

B. Agency personnel offices.

C. State employment offices.

D. *Federal Career Opportunities/Federal Jobs Digest*

E. Federal Job Opportunities Bulletin Boards.

V. Begin preparing the application packet.

A. Get *X-118 Qualification Standards* for the target job.

B. If more information is needed, get *Position Classification Standards* for the target job.

C. Examine announcement; are additional forms needed?

D. If not already prepared, make a "master" SF 171/OF 612 for the target series and grade.

E. Call for more information about the vacancy.

VI. Prepare a "Mail-in" packet.

A. Make a **clear** copy of the master SF 171 or OF 612 and fill in unfilled blocks, including block 1 and your signature and date.

B. Prepare the supplemental forms (race and sex surveys, SF 15, KSAO sheets, etc.).

C. Make a photo copy of the completed packet.

D. Mail the application packet and complete a log record.

VII. Follow-through.

A. Call the POC a few days later and ask:

1. Whether the packet arrived.

2. Has anything changed regarding that vacancy?

3. What timetable will be followed in rating the applications and sending ratings to hiring officials?

B. Based on the timetable given by the POC, call later to find out if you were rated.

1. If you were not rated, ask why not.

2. If your application was misread, ask to appeal the rating.

3. Again ask for timetable and other information about this vacancy.

C. If rated, call back every two weeks and ask:

1. Has the application gone to the hiring activity?

2. Has anything changed regarding the vacancy?

D. If not selected, call the POC and ask why.

E. Update the log records.

STANDARD FORMS

S everal standard U.S. government forms are reproduced here, including

- *SF 171, Application for Federal Employment* used
to apply for federal jobs

- *SF 171-A, Continuation Sheet for SF 171* used to
describe additional work experience

- *Supplemental Information Sheet for SF 171* a form
to use when the information will not fit a block on
the SF 171 (this is not a government form)

- *SF 172, Amendment to Application for Federal*

Employment used by current federal employees to
update their records or to amend an SF 171 (conditions having changed since it was submitted for a
vacancy).

- *OF 612, Optional Application for Federal Employment* used in place of the SF 171 as the heart of an
  application packet.

- *Work Experience Continuation Sheet for OF 612*
  used with OF 612 to list more jobs, or provide more
  details about jobs and work experience.

- *OF 306, Declaration for Federal Employment* is a
  form that may be requested by the hiring agency
  from applicants who use OF 612 or a resume as the
  core of their application packet. This is not used
  with an SF 171.

- *OPM Form 1170/17, List of College Courses* a form
  to use to record your college background if a
  course listing is required.

- *SF 15, Application for 10-Point Veteran Preference*
  used by veterans and certain relatives of veterans
  to claim the ten point veterans' preferential treatment when being rated for a federal job. Also
  includes additional information on eligibility for
  veterans preference and the special program for
  Vietnam Era vets.

- *Application Package Log Sheet* is a way to keep
  track of an SF 171 application packet.

SF 171, Application for Federal Employment

The SF 171 will be the centerpiece in any application package. See Chapter Five for guidance on how to write a strong SF 171. The copies of the form on the following pages may be reproduced and submitted as part of an application.

Application for Federal Employment—SF 171

Read the instructions before you complete this application. *Type or print clearly in dark ink.*

Form Approved:
OMB No. 3206-0012

GENERAL INFORMATION

1 What kind of job are you applying for? *Give title and announcement no. (if any)*

2 Social Security Number

3 Sex
☐ Male ☐ Female

4 Birth date *(Month, Day, Year)*

5 Birthplace *(City and State or Country)*

6 Name *(Last, First, Middle)*

Mailing address *(include apartment number, if any)*

City   State   ZIP Code

7 Other names ever used *(e.g., maiden name, nickname, etc.)*

8 Home Phone
Area Code | Number

9 Work Phone
Area Code | Number | Extension

10 Were you ever employed as a civilian by the Federal Government? If **"NO"**, go to **Item 11.** If **"YES"**, mark each type of job you held with an **"X"**.

☐ Temporary   ☐ Career-Conditional   ☐ Career   ☐ Excepted

What is your **highest** grade, classification series and job title?

Dates at **highest** grade: FROM   TO

FOR USE OF EXAMINING OFFICE ONLY

Date entered register

Form reviewed:
Form approved:

Option	Grade	Earned Rating	Veteran Preference	Augmented Rating
			☐ No Preference Claimed	
			☐ 5 Points (Tentative)	
			☐ 10 Pts. (30% Or More Comp. Dis.)	
			☐ 10 Pts. (Less Than 30% Comp. Dis.)	
			☐ Other 10 Points	

Initials and Date

☐ Disallowed   ☐ Being Investigated

FOR USE OF APPOINTING OFFICE ONLY

Preference has been verified through proof that the separation was under honorable conditions, and other proof as required.

☐ 5-Point   ☐ 10-Point--30% or More Compensable Disability   ☐ 10-Point--Less Than 30% Compensable Disability   ☐ 10-Point--Other

Signature and Title

Agency   Date

AVAILABILITY

11 When can you start work? *(Month and Year)*

12 What is the **lowest** pay you will accept? *(You will not be considered for jobs which pay less than you indicate.)*
Pay $ _____ per _____ OR Grade _____

13 In what geographic area(s) are you willing to work?

14 Are you willing to work:	YES	NO
A. 40 hours per week *(full-time)?*		
B. 25-32 hours per week *(part-time)?*		
C. 17-24 hours per week *(part-time)?*		
D. 16 or fewer hours per week *(part-time)?*		
E. An intermittent job *(on-call/seasonal)?*		
F. Weekends, shifts, or rotating shifts?		

15 Are you willing to take a temporary job lasting:		
A. 5 to 12 months *(sometimes longer)?*		
B. 1 to 4 months?		
C. Less than 1 month?		

16 Are you willing to travel away from home for:		
A. 1 to 5 nights each month?		
B. 6 to 10 nights each month?		
C. 11 or more nights each month?		

MILITARY SERVICE AND VETERAN PREFERENCE

17 Have you served in the United States Military Service? *If your only active duty was training in the Reserves or National Guard, answer "NO". If* **"NO"**, *go to item 22.*	YES	NO

18 Did you or will you retire at or above the rank of major or lieutenant commander?		

MILITARY SERVICE AND VETERAN PREFERENCE *(Cont.)*

19 Were you discharged from the military service under honorable conditions? *(If your discharge was changed to "honorable" or "general" by a Discharge Review Board, answer "YES". If you received a clemency discharge, answer "NO".)* If **"NO"**, provide below the date and type of discharge you received.	YES	NO

Discharge Date *(Month, Day, Year)*	Type of Discharge

20 List the dates *(Month, Day, Year)*, and branch for all **active duty** military service.

From	To	Branch of Service

21 If all your active military duty was after October 14, 1976, list the full names and dates of all campaign badges or expeditionary medals you received or were entitled to receive.

22 Read the instructions that came with this form before completing this item. When you have determined your eligibility for veteran preference from the instructions, place an **"X"** in the box next to your veteran preference claim.

☐ NO PREFERENCE

☐ 5-POINT PREFERENCE -- You must show proof when you are hired.

10-POINT PREFERENCE -- If you claim 10-point preference, place an **"X"** in the box below next to the basis for your claim. **To receive 10-point preference you must also complete a Standard Form 15, Application for 10-Point Veteran Preference, which is available from any Federal Job Information Center. ATTACH THE COMPLETED SF 15 AND REQUESTED PROOF TO THIS APPLICATION.**

☐ Non-compensably disabled or Purple Heart recipient.

☐ Compensably disabled, less than 30 percent.

☐ Spouse, widow(er), or mother of a deceased or disabled veteran.

☐ Compensably disabled, 30 percent or more.

THE FEDERAL GOVERNMENT IS AN EQUAL OPPORTUNITY EMPLOYER
PREVIOUS EDITION USABLE UNTIL 12-31-90

NSN 7540-00-935-7150   171-110

Standard Form 171 (Rev. 6-88)
U.S. Office of Personnel Management
FPM Chapter 295

Page 1

WORK EXPERIENCE *If you have no work experience, write "NONE" in A below and go to 25 on page 3.*

23 May we ask your present employer about your character, qualifications, and work record? *A "NO" will not affect our review of your qualifications. If you answer "NO" and we need to contact your present employer before we can offer you a job, we will contact you first.* . . . . | **YES** | **NO** |

24 READ **WORK EXPERIENCE** IN THE INSTRUCTIONS BEFORE YOU BEGIN.

- Describe your current or most recent job in Block **A** and work backwards, describing each job you held **during the past 10 years.** If you were **unemployed** for longer than **3 months** within the past 10 years, list the dates and your address(es) in an experience block.

- You may sum up in one block work that you did **more than 10 years ago.** But if that work **is related** to the type of job you are applying for, describe each related job in a separate block.

- INCLUDE VOLUNTEER WORK *(non-paid work)*--**If the work** *(or a part of the work)* **is like the job you are applying for,** complete **all** parts of the experience block just as you would for a paying job. You may receive credit for work experience with religious, community, welfare, service, and other organizations.

- INCLUDE MILITARY SERVICE--You should complete **all** parts of the experience block just as you would for a non-military job, including all supervisory experience. Describe each major change of duties or responsibilities in a separate experience block.

- IF YOU NEED MORE SPACE TO DESCRIBE A JOB--Use sheets of paper the same size as this page (be sure to include **all** information we ask for in **A** and **B** below). On **each** sheet show your name, Social Security Number, and the announcement number or job title.

- IF YOU NEED MORE EXPERIENCE BLOCKS, use the SF 171-A or a sheet of paper.

- IF YOU NEED TO UPDATE (ADD MORE RECENT JOBS), use the SF 172 or a sheet of paper as described above.

A | Name and address of employer's organization *(include ZIP Code, if known)* | Dates employed *(give month, day and year)* | Average number if hours per week | Number of employees you supervise |
From:	To:		
Salary or earnings		Your reason for wanting to leave
Starting $	per	
Ending $	per	

| Your immediate supervisor | | | Exact title of your job | If Federal employment *(civilian or military)* list series, grade or rank, and, if promoted in this job, the date of your last promotion |
| Name | Area Code | Telephone No. | | |

Description of work: Describe your specific duties, responsibilities and accomplishments in this job, **including** the job title(s) of any employees you supervise. *If you describe more than one type of work (for example, carpentry and painting, or personnel and budget), write the approximate percentage of time you spent doing each.*

For Agency Use (skill codes, etc.)

B | Name and address of employer's organization *(include ZIP Code, if known)* | Dates employed *(give month, day and year)* | Average number of hours per week | Number of employees you supervised |
From:	To:		
Salary or earnings		Your reason for leaving
Starting $	per	
Ending $	per	

| Your immediate supervisor | | | Exact title of your job | If Federal employment *(civilian or military)* list series, grade or rank, and, if promoted in this job, the date of your last promotion |
| Name | Area Code | Telephone No. | | |

Description of work: Describe your specific duties, responsibilities and accomplishments in this job, **including** the job title(s) of any employees you supervised. *If you describe more than one type of work (for example, carpentry and painting, or personnel and budget), write the approximate percentage of time you spent doing each.*

For Agency Use (skill codes, etc.)

← ATTACH ANY ADDITIONAL FORMS AND SHEETS HERE

EDUCATION

25 Did you graduate from high school? *If you have a GED high school equivalency or will graduate within the next nine months, answer "YES".*

26 Write the name and location *(city and state)* of the last high school you attended or where you obtained your GED high school equivalency.

YES ☐   If "YES", give month and year graduated or received GED equivalency: ....
NO ☐   If "NO", give the highest grade you completed: .

27 Have you ever attended college or graduate school?   YES ☐   If "YES", continue with 28.   NO ☐   If "NO", go to 31.

28 NAME AND LOCATION *(city, state and ZIP Code)* OF COLLEGE OR UNIVERSITY.. *If you expect to graduate within nine months, give the month and year you expect to receive your degree:*

Name	City	State	ZIP Code	From	To	Semester	Quarter	TYPE OF DEGREE (e.g. B.A., M.A.)	MONTH AND YEAR OF DEGREE
1)									
2)									
3)									

(MONTH AND YEAR ATTENDED / NUMBER OF CREDIT HOURS COMPLETED)

29 CHIEF UNDERGRADUATE SUBJECTS *Show major on the first line*

	NUMBER OF CREDIT HOURS COMPLETED Semester	Quarter
1)		
2)		
3)		

30 CHIEF GRADUATE SUBJECTS *Show major on the first line*

	NUMBER OF CREDIT HOURS COMPLETED Semester	Quarter
1)		
2)		
3)		

31 If you have completed any **other courses or training related to the kind of jobs you are applying for** *(trade, vocational, Armed Forces, business)* give information below.

NAME AND LOCATION *(city, state and ZIP Code)* OF SCHOOL	From	To	CLASS-ROOM HOURS	SUBJECT(S)	TRAINING COMPLETED YES NO
1) School Name / City State ZIP Code					
2) School Name / City State ZIP Code					

SPECIAL SKILLS, ACCOMPLISHMENTS AND AWARDS

32 Give the title and year of any honors, awards or fellowships you have received. List your special qualifications, skills or accomplishments that may help you get a job. *Some examples are: skills with computers or other machines; most important publications (do not submit copies); public speaking and writing experience; membership in professional or scientific societies; patents or inventions; etc.*

33 How many words per minute can you: TYPE? TAKE DICTATION? *Agencies may test your skills before hiring you.*

34 List **job-related** licenses or certificates that you have, such as: *registered nurse; lawyer; radio operator; driver's; pilot's; etc.*

LICENSE OR CERTIFICATE	DATE OF LATEST LICENSE OR CERTIFICATE	STATE OR OTHER LICENSING AGENCY
1)		
2)		

35 Do you speak or read a language other than English *(include sign language)?* **Applicants for jobs that require a language other than English may be given an interview conducted solely in that language.**   YES ☐   NO ☐   If "YES", list each language and place an "X" in each column that applies to you. If "NO", go to 36.

LANGUAGE(S)	CAN PREPARE AND GIVE LECTURES Fluently	With Difficulty	CAN SPEAK AND UNDERSTAND Fluently	Passably	CAN TRANSLATE ARTICLES Into English	From English	CAN READ ARTICLES FOR OWN USE Easily	With Difficulty
1)								
2)								

REFERENCES

36 List three people who are not related to you and are not supervisors you listed under **24** who know your qualifications and fitness for the kind of job for which you are applying. At least **one** should know you well on a personal basis.

FULL NAME OF REFERENCE	TELEPHONE NUMBER(S) (Include Area Code)	PRESENT BUSINESS OR HOME ADDRESS (Number, street and city)	STATE	ZIP CODE
1)				
2)				
3)				

Page 3

BACKGROUND INFORMATION-- *You must answer each question in this section before we can process your application.*

37 Are you a citizen of the United States? *(In most cases you must be a U.S. citizen to be hired. You will be required to submit proof of identity and citizenship at the time you are hired.)* If **"NO"**, give the country or countries you are a citizen of: _____ | YES | NO |

NOTE: It is important that you give complete and truthful answers to questions 38 through 44. If you answer **"YES"** to any of them, provide your explanation(s) in **Item 45. Include** convictions resulting from a plea of nolo contendere *(no contest).* **Omit:** 1) traffic fines of $100.00 or less; 2) any violation of law committed before your 16th birthday; 3) any violation of law committed before your 18th birthday, if finally decided in juvenile court or under a Youth Offender law; 4) any conviction set aside under the Federal Youth Corrections Act or similar State law; 5) any conviction whose record was expunged under Federal or State law. We will consider the date, facts, and circumstances of each event you list. In most cases you can still be considered for Federal jobs. However, **if you fail to tell the truth or fail to list all relevant** events or circumstances, this may be grounds for not hiring you, for firing you after you begin work, or for criminal prosecution (18 USC 1001).

38 During the last **10 years**, were you **fired from any job** for any reason, did you **quit after being told that you would be fired,** or did you leave by mutual agreement because of specific problems?. . . . . | YES | NO |

39 Have you **ever** been convicted of, or forfeited collateral for **any felony violation?** *(Generally, a felony is defined as any violation of law punishable by imprisonment of longer than one year, except for violations called misdemeanors under State law which are punishable by imprisonment of two years or less.)* . . . .

40 Have you **ever** been convicted of, or forfeited collateral for **any firearms or explosives violation?** . . . .

41 Are you **now** under charges for **any** violation of law? . . . .

42 During the **last 10 years** have you forfeited collateral, been convicted, been imprisoned, been on probation, or been on parole? Do **not** include violations reported in 39, 40, or 41, above. . . . .

43 Have you **ever** been convicted by a military **court-martial?** If no military service, answer **"NO"**. . . . .

44 Are you **delinquent** on any Federal debt? *(Include delinquencies arising from Federal taxes, loans, overpayment of benefits, and other debts to the U.S. Government **plus** defaults on Federally guaranteed or insured loans such as student and home mortgage loans.)* . . . . . .

45 If **"YES"** in: 38 - Explain for each job the problem(s) and your reason(s) for leaving. Give the employer's name and address.
39 through 43 - Explain each violation. Give place of occurrence and name/address of police or court involved.
44 - Explain the type, length and amount of the delinquency or default, and steps you are taking to correct errors or repay the debt. Give any identification number associated with the debt and the address of the Federal agency involved.
NOTE: If you need more space, use a sheet of paper, and include the item number.

Item No.	Date (Mo./Yr.)	Explanation	Mailing Address
			Name of Employer, Police, Court, or Federal Agency
			City State ZIP Code
			Name of Employer, Police, Court, or Federal Agency
			City State ZIP Code

46 Do you receive, or have you ever applied for retirement pay, pension, or other pay based on military, Federal civilian, or District of Columbia Government service? . . . . | YES | NO |

47 Do any of your relatives work for the United States Government or the United States Armed Forces? Include: *father; mother; husband; wife; son; daughter; brother; sister; uncle; aunt; first cousin; nephew; niece; father-in-law; mother-in-law; son-in-law; daughter-in-law; brother-in-law; sister-in-law; stepfather; stepmother; stepson; stepdaughter; stepbrother; stepsister; half brother; and half sister.* . . . .
If **"YES"**, provide details below. If you need more space, use a sheet of paper.

Name	Relationship	Department, Agency or Branch of Armed Forces

SIGNATURE, CERTIFICATION, AND RELEASE OF INFORMATION

YOU MUST SIGN THIS APPLICATION.   Read the following carefully before you sign.

- A false statement on any part of your application may be grounds for not hiring you, or for firing you after you begin work. Also, you may be punished by fine or imprisonment (U.S. Code, title 18, section 1001).
- If you are a male born after December 31, 1959 you must be registered with the Selective Service System or have a valid exemption in order to be eligible for Federal employment. You will be required to certify as to your status at the time of appointment.
- **I understand** that any information I give may be investigated as allowed by law or Presidential order.
- **I consent** to the release of information about my ability and fitness for Federal employment **by** *employers, schools, law enforcement agencies and other individuals and organizations,* **to** *investigators, personnel staffing specialists, and other authorized employees of the Federal Government.*
- **I certify** that, to the best of my knowledge and belief, **all** of my statements are true, correct, complete, and made in good faith.

48 SIGNATURE *(Sign each application in dark ink)* | **49** DATE SIGNED *(Month, day, year)*

SF 171-A, Continuation Sheet for SF 171

This form is used to list additional jobs and other work experiences. As explained in Chapter Five, use one block for each job or work experience which is relevant to the target job, starting with your current job and working back roughly ten years. The first job listed on a continuation sheet should be put into the top half of the page and the block should be labelled "C".

The copies of the form on the following page may be reproduced and submitted as part of an application.

Standard Form 171-A— *Continuation Sheet for SF 171*

• Attach all SF 171-A's to your application at the top of page 3.

Form Approved:
OMB No. 3206-0012

1. Name *(Last, First, Middle Initial)*	2. Social Security Number

3. Job Title or Announcement Number You Are Applying For	4. Date Completed

ADDITIONAL WORK EXPERIENCE BLOCKS

□ Name and address of employer's organization *(include ZIP Code, if known)*

Dates employed *(give month, day and year)*

From: To:

Salary or earnings

Starting $ per

Ending $ per

Average number of hours per week

Number of employees you supervised

Your reason for leaving

Your immediate supervisor			Exact title of your job	If Federal employment *(civilian or military)* list series, grade or rank, and, if promoted in this job, the date of your last promotion
Name	Area Code	Telephone No.		

Description of work: Describe your specific duties, responsibilities and accomplishments in this job, **including** the job title(s) of any employees you supervised. *If you describe more than one type of work (for example, carpentry and painting, or personnel and budget), write the approximate percentage of time you spent doing each.*

For Agency Use (skill codes, etc.)

□ Name and address of employer's organization *(include ZIP Code, if known)*

Dates employed *(give month, day and year)*

From: To:

Salary or earnings

Starting $ per

Ending $ per

Average number of hours per week

Number of employees you supervised

Your reason for leaving

Your immediate supervisor			Exact title of your job	If Federal employment *(civilian or military)* list series, grade or rank, and, if promoted in this job, the date of your last promotion
Name	Area Code	Telephone No.		

Description of work: Describe your specific duties, responsibilities and accomplishments in this job, **including** the job title(s) of any employees you supervised. *If you describe more than one type of work (for example, carpentry and painting, or personnel and budget), write the approximate percentage of time you spent doing each.*

For Agency Use (skill codes, etc.)

THE FEDERAL GOVERNMENT IS AN EQUAL OPPORTUNITY EMPLOYER

PREVIOUS EDITION USABLE

Standard Form 171-A (Rev. 6-83)
U.S. Office of Personnel Management
FPM Chapter 295

Supplemental Information Sheet for SF 171

Some of the blocks on the SF 171 and the SF 171-A Continuation Sheet do not provide enough space for adequate descriptions. Make copies of the form on the next page and use it to provide additional information. Each block you describe on this form should be clearly marked (see the examples) so the reviewer will know which blocks are being given more space. Be sure to review the examples in Appendix J.

SUPPLEMENTAL INFORMATION SHEET FOR SF 171

SUPPLEMENTAL INFORMATION:

1. Name (Last, First, Middle Initial)	2. SSN
3. Job Title/Announcement Number	4.Date

SF 172, Amendment to Application For Federal Employment

This form can be used by current federal employees to update their personnel records. The form can also be used if you have applied for a position, no decision has yet been made about your application, and things in your life have changed since you submitted your application package. You may complete this form and send it to the same place your sent your application and request that the new information be added to your application. The information that has to be put into the blocks on this form is identical to the information required on comparable blocks of the SF 171.

Copies of the form on the next two pages may be made and submitted.

Standard Form 172 – Amendment to Application for Federal Employment – SF 171

Form Approved:
OMB No. 3206-0002
Approval Expires 10-31-87

Read the following instructions before you complete this application. Type or print clearly in dark ink.

- You may use this form to update your Application for Federal Employment (SF 171) if you have had 2 or fewer new jobs since you completed your last SF 171.
- You must submit a new SF 171 if you have previously updated your application or have three or more new jobs.
- Federal agencies must accept your previously completed SF 171 as current when this form or a signed photocopy is attached.

GENERAL INFORMATION

1 Reason for updating SF 171 (Check one:)

☐ To update my SF 171 for _____
(Indicate position title or announcement number)

☐ To update SF 171 in my Official Personnel Folder.

☐ To update attached SF 171. ☐ As requested.

2 Name (Last, First, Middle)

Street address or RFD number (include apartment number, if any)

City   State   ZIP Code

3 Birth date (Month, Day, Year)

4 Social Security Number

5 What is the lowest pay or grade you will accept?

Pay $ per   OR Grade

6 Name on SF 171 being amended, if different from **2**

7 May we ask your present employer about your character, qualifications and work record? A "NO" will not affect our review of your qualifications. If you answer "NO" and we need to contact your present employer before we can offer you a job, we will contact you first.......................

YES	NO

WORK EXPERIENCE   If you have no new work experience, write "NONE" in A below and go to 9 on page 2

8
- Describe your current or most recent job or volunteer experience in Block A and work backwards, describing up to 2 periods of experience not on your SF 171.
- If you were **unemployed** for longer than **3 months**, list the dates and your address(es) at that time in **10**.

A

Name and address of employer's organization (include ZIP Code, if known)	Dates employed (give month and year) From: To:	Average number of hours per week
	Salary or earnings Starting $ per Ending $ per	Place of employment City State

Exact title of your job	Name of immediate supervisor	Area Code Telephone Number	Number and titles of employees you supervised

Kind of business or organization (manufacturing, accounting, social service, etc.)	If Federal employment (civilian or military), list: series, grade or rank, and the date of your last promotion	Your reason for wanting to leave

Description of work: Describe your specific duties, responsibilities and accomplishments in this job. If you describe more than one type of work (for example, carpentry and painting or personnel and budget), write the approximate percentage of time you spent doing each.

For Agency Use (skill codes, etc.)

PREVIOUS EDITION USABLE

NSN 7540-00-142-8756

172-105

Standard Form 172 (Rev. 3/84)
Office of Personnel Management
FPM Chapter 295

B	Name and address of employer's organization (include ZIP Code, if known)	Dates employed (give month and year) From: To:	Average number of hours per week
		Salary or earnings Starting $ per Ending $ per	Place of employment City State

Exact title of your job | **Name of immediate supervisor** | **Area Code Telephone Number** | **Number and titles of employees you supervised**

Kind of business or organization (manufacturing, accounting, social service, etc.) | **If Federal employment** (civilian or military), list: series, grade or rank, and the date of your last promotion | **Reason for leaving**

Description of work: Describe your specific duties, responsibilities and accomplishments in this job. If you describe more than one type of work (for example, carpentry and painting or personnel and budget), write the approximate percentage of time you spent doing each.

For Agency Use (skill codes, etc.)

OTHER CHANGES OR ADDITIONS AND ADDITIONAL SPACE

9 Does any other information on your SF 171 need updating (for example, telephone number, education, or special skills)? .... **YES** ▷ Provide updated information in **10**. **NO** ▷ Go to **11** and **12**.

10 Write the number to which each answer applies. If you need more space, use sheets of paper the same size as this page. On each sheet write your name and Social Security Number. Attach all sheets to this form.

SIGNATURE, CERTIFICATION, AND RELEASE OF INFORMATION   For Privacy Act Statement See SF 171

YOU MUST SIGN THIS APPLICATION. Read the following carefully before you sign.

A false statement on any part of your application or this amendment may be grounds for not hiring you, or for firing you after you begin work. Also, you may be punished by fine or imprisonment (U.S. Code, Title 18, Section 1001).

   I understand that any information I give may be investigated as allowed by law or Presidential order;

   I consent to the release of information about my ability and fitness for Federal employment by employers, schools, law enforcement agencies and other individuals and organizations, to investigators, personnel staffing specialists, and other authorized employees of the Federal Government.

   I certify that, to the best of my knowledge and belief, all statements on my SF 171 and SF 172 are correct, complete, and made in good faith.

11 Signature (Sign in dark ink) | **12** Date Signed (Month, day, year)

Form Approved
OMB No. 3206-0219

OPTIONAL APPLICATION FOR FEDERAL EMPLOYMENT - OF 612

You may apply for most jobs with a resume, this form, or other written format. If your resume or application does not provide all the information requested on this form and in the job vacancy announcement, you may lose consideration for a job.

1 Job title in announcement

2 Grade(s) applying for

3 Announcement number

4 Last name   First and middle names

5 Social Security Number

6 Mailing address

City   State   ZIP Code

7 Phone numbers (include area code)

Daytime

Evening

WORK EXPERIENCE

8 Describe your paid and nonpaid work experience related to the job for which you are applying. Do **not** attach job descriptions.

1) Job title (if Federal, include series and grade)

From (MM/YY)   To (MM/YY)   Salary   per   Hours per week
                                                  $

Employer's name and address   Supervisor's name and phone number

Describe your duties and accomplishments

2) Job title (if Federal, include series and grade)

From (MM/YY)   To (MM/YY)   Salary   per   Hours per week
                                                  $

Employer's name and address   Supervisor's name and phone number

Describe your duties and accomplishments

50612-101   NSN 7540-01-351-9178   Optional Form 612 (September 1994)
                                                                           U.S. Office of Personnel Management

9 May we contact your current supervisor?

YES [   ]   NO [   ]► If we need to contact your current supervisor before making an offer, we will contact you first.

EDUCATION

10 Mark highest level completed. **Some HS** [   ]   **HS/GED** [   ]   **Associate** [   ]   **Bachelor** [   ]   **Master** [   ]   **Doctoral** [   ]

11 Last high school (HS) or GED school. Give the school's name, city, State, ZIP Code (if known), and year diploma or GED received.

12 Colleges and universities attended. Do **not** attach a copy of your transcript unless requested.

	Name	Total Credits Earned Semester Quarter	Major(s)	Degree - Year (if any) Received
1)	City	State ZIP Code		
2)				
3)				

OTHER QUALIFICATIONS

13 **Job-related** training courses (give title and year). **Job-related** skills (other languages, computer software/hardware, tools, machinery, typing speed, etc.). **Job-related** certificates and licenses (current only). **Job-related** honors, awards, and special accomplishments (publications, memberships in professional/honor societies, leadership activities, public speaking, and performance awards). Give dates, but do **not** send documents unless requested.

GENERAL

14 Are you a U.S. citizen?   YES [   ]   NO [   ]► Give the country of your citizenship.

15 Do you claim veterans' preference? **NO** [   ]   **YES** [   ]► Mark your claim of 5 or 10 points below.
  5 points [   ]► Attach your DD 214 or other proof. **10 points** [   ]► Attach an *Application for 10-Point Veterans' Preference* (SF 15) and proof required.

16 Were you ever a Federal civilian employee?   Series   Grade   From (MM/YY)   To (MM/YY)
                                        NO [   ]   **YES** [   ]► For highest civilian grade give:

17 Are you eligible for reinstatement based on career or career-conditional Federal status?
                                        NO [   ]   **YES** [   ]► If requested, attach SF 50 proof.

APPLICANT CERTIFICATION

18 I **certify** that, to the best of my knowledge and belief, all of the information on and attached to this application is true, correct, complete and made in good faith. **I understand** that false or fraudulent information on or attached to this application may be grounds for not hiring me or for firing me after I begin work, and may be punishable by fine or imprisonment. **I understand** that any information I give may be investigated.

SIGNATURE   **DATE SIGNED**

Continuation of Page 1

(Alternate) Work Experience Continuation for OF-612

1 Job title in announcement		2 Grade(s) applying for	3 Announcement number
4 Last name	First and middle names		5 Social Security Number

WORK EXPERIENCE continued

Job title (if Federal, include series and grade)

From (MM/YY)	To (MM/YY)	Salary $	per	Hours per week
Employer's name and address				Supervisor's name and phone number ( )

Describe your duties and accomplishments

Continuation of Page 1

(Alternate) Work Experience Continuation for OF-612

1 Job title in announcement			2 Grade(s) applying for	3 Announcement number
4 Last name	First and middle names			5 Social Security Number

WORK EXPERIENCE continued

Job title (if Federal, include series and grade)

From (MM/YY)	To (MM/YY)	Salary $	per	Hours per week
Employer's name and address				Supervisor's name and phone number ( )

Describe your duties and accomplishments

Job title (if Federal, include series and grade)

From (MM/YY)	To (MM/YY)	Salary $	per	Hours per week
Employer's name and address				Supervisor's name and phone number ( )

Describe your duties and accomplishments

General Purpose Continuation for OF-612

1 Job title in announcement		2 Grade(s) applying for	3 Announcement number
4 Last name	First and middle names		5 Social Security Number

ADDITIONAL SPACE FOR OF-612 ANSWERS

ITEM NO.	RESPONSE

This form produced by Federal Research Service, Inc., Vienna Virginia

Optional Form 306
September 1994
U.S. Office of Personnel
Management

Declaration for Federal Employment

Form Approved:
O.M.B. No. 3206-0182
NSN 7540-01-368-7775
50306-101

GENERAL INFORMATION

1 FULL NAME
▶

2 SOCIAL SECURITY NUMBER
▶

3 PLACE OF BIRTH *(Include City and State or Country)*
▶

4 DATE OF BIRTH *(MM/DD/YY)*
▶

5 OTHER NAMES EVER USED *(For example, maiden name, nickname, etc.)*
▶
▶

6 PHONE NUMBERS *(Include Area Codes)*
DAY ▶
NIGHT ▶

MILITARY SERVICE

	Yes	No

7 Have you served in the United States Military Service? *If your only active duty was training in the Reserves or National Guard, answer "NO".*

If you answered "YES", list the branch, dates (MM/DD/YY), and type of discharge for all active duty military service.

BRANCH	FROM	TO	TYPE OF DISCHARGE

BACKGROUND INFORMATION

For all questions, provide all additional requested information under item 15 or on attached sheets. The circumstances of each event you list will be considered. However, in most cases you can still be considered for Federal jobs.

For questions 8, 9, and 10, your answers should include convictions resulting from a plea of nolo contendere *(no contest)*, but omit (1) traffic fines of $300 or less, (2) any violation of law committed before your 16th birthday, (3) any violation of law committed before your 18th birthday if finally decided in juvenile court or under a Youth Offender law, (4) any conviction set aside under the Federal Youth Corrections Act or similar State law, and (5) any conviction whose record was expunged under Federal or State law.

8 During the last 10 years, have you been convicted, been imprisoned, been on probation, or been on parole? (Includes felonies, firearms or explosives violations, misdemeanors, and all other offenses.) *If "Yes", use item 15 to provide the date, explanation of the violation, place of occurrence, and the name and address of the police department or court involved.*

9 Have you been convicted by a military court-martial in the past 10 years? (If no military service, answer "NO".) *If "Yes", use item 15 to provide the date, explanation of the violation, place of occurrence, and the name and address of the military authority or court involved.*

10 Are you now under charges for any violation of law? *If "Yes", use item 15 to provide the date, explanation of the violation, place of occurrence, and the name and address of the police department or court involved.*

11 During the last 5 years, were you fired from any job for any reason, did you quit after being told that you would be fired, did you leave any job by mutual agreement because of specific problems, or were you debarred from Federal employment by the Office of Personnel Management? *If "Yes", use item 15 to provide the date, an explanation of the problem and reason for leaving, and the employer's name and address.*

12 Are you delinquent on any Federal debt? (Includes delinquencies arising from Federal taxes, loans, overpayment of benefits, and other debts to the U.S. Government, plus defaults of Federally guaranteed or insured loans such as student and home mortgage loans.) *If "Yes", use item 15 to provide the type, length, and amount of the delinquency or default, and steps that you are taking to correct the error or repay the debt.*

ADDITIONAL QUESTIONS

13 Do any of your relatives work for the agency or organization to which you are submitting this form? (Includes father, mother, husband, wife, son, daughter, brother, sister, uncle, aunt, first cousin, nephew, niece, father-in-law, mother-in-law, son-in-law, daughter-in-law, brother-in-law, sister-in-law, stepfather, stepmother, stepson, stepdaughter, stepbrother, stepsister, half brother, and half sister.) *If "Yes", use item 15 to provide the name, relationship, and the Department, Agency, or Branch of the Armed Forces for which your relative works.*

14 Do you receive, or have you ever applied for, retirement pay, pension, or other pay based on military, Federal civilian, or District of Columbia Government service?

CONTINUATION SPACE / AGENCY OPTIONAL QUESTIONS

15 Provide details requested in items 8 through 13 and 17c in the continuation space below or on attached sheets. Be sure to identify attached sheets with your name, Social Security Number, and item number, and to include ZIP Codes in all addresses. If any questions are printed below, please answer as instructed (these questions are specific to your position, and your agency is authorized to ask them).

CERTIFICATIONS / ADDITIONAL QUESTION

APPLICANT: If you are applying for a position and have not yet been selected. Carefully review your answers on this form and any attached sheets. When this form and all attached materials are accurate, complete item 16/16a.

APPOINTEE: If you are being appointed. Carefully review your answers on this form and any attached sheets, including any other application materials that your agency has attached to this form. If any information requires correction to be accurate as of the date you are signing, make changes on this form or the attachments and/or provide updated information on additional sheets, initialing and dating all changes and additions. When this form and all attached materials are accurate, complete item 16/16b and answer item 17.

16 I certify that, to the best of my knowledge and belief, all of the information on and attached to this Declaration for Federal Employment, including any attached application materials, is true, correct, complete, and made in good faith. I understand that a false or fraudulent answer to any question on any part of this declaration or its attachments may be grounds for not hiring me, or for firing me after I begin work, and may be punishable by fine or imprisonment. I understand that any information I give may be investigated for purposes of determining eligibility for Federal employment as allowed by law or Presidential order. I consent to the release of information about my ability and fitness for Federal employment by *employers, schools, law enforcement agencies,* and *other individuals and organizations* to *investigators, personnel specialists,* and *other authorized employees of the Federal Government.* I understand that for financial or lending institutions, medical institutions, hospitals, health care professionals, and some other sources of information, a separate specific release may be needed, and I may be contacted for such a release at a later date.

16a Applicant's Signature ▶
(Sign in ink)   Date ▶

16b Appointee's Signature ▶
(Sign in ink)   Date ▶   APPOINTING OFFICER: Enter Date of Appointment or Conversion ▶

17 **Appointee Only (*Respond only if you have been employed by the Federal Government before*):** Your elections of life insurance during previous Federal employment may affect your eligibility for life insurance during your new appointment. These questions are asked to help your personnel office make a correct determination.

	Date (MM/DD/YY)		
17a When did you leave your last Federal job?			
	Yes	No	Don't Know
17b When you worked for the Federal Government the last time, did you waive Basic Life Insurance or any type of optional life insurance? · · · · · · · · · · · · · · · · · · ·			
17c If you answered "Yes" to item 17b, did you later cancel the waiver(s)? *If your answer to item 17c is "No," use item 15 to identify the type(s) of insurance for which waivers were not cancelled.*			

OPM Form 1170/17, List of College Courses

The form on the next few pages can be used to submit copies of your educational transcript(s) if you are applying for a position which has positive educational requirements (for example, if the announcement says you must have a certain number of college semester hours in mathematics or other subjects). For your application, you can tape a copy of your educational transcript to copies of the form. If accepted for the position, the personnel office will require an official copy of all transcripts.

The forms on the next few pages may be reproduced as needed.

STANDARD FORMS   173

SUPPLEMENTAL QUALIFICATIONS STATEMENT

LIST OF COLLEGE COURSES AND CERTIFICATE OF SCHOLASTIC ACHIEVEMENT

Complete and submit this Form with your Application for Federal Employment or as instructed.

Form Approved
OMB No. 3206-0038

1. Name (Last, First, M.I.)	2. Birth date (Month, day, year)	3. Social Security Number

4. Position for which you are applying (Include options, if any)

5. List the undergraduate and/or graduate college degrees you have received or expect to receive (Give name of degree, name of college or university granting degree, and date received or to be received)

6. State your major undergraduate course(s) of study	6a. State your major graduate course(s) of study

PART I — COLLEGE COURSES

List below by appropriate academic field (e.g., biology, mechanical engineering, economics, sociology, etc.) all courses you have taken (including those failed) which appear to satisfy the qualification requirements of positions for which you are applying. List graduate and undergraduate courses separately. Credits for each category should be totaled to determine if you meet the minimum course requirements.

Indicate academic field:

Indicate academic field:

DESCRIPTIVE TITLE	COMPLE-TION DATE	GRADE	SEM	QTR	CLASS ROOM	DESCRIPTIVE TITLE	COMPLE-TION DATE	GRADE	SEM	QTR	CLASS ROOM

TOTAL / TOTAL

U.S. Office of Personnel Management

OPM 1170/17 (Rev. 4/90)

Indicate academic field:

DESCRIPTIVE TITLE	COMPLE-TION DATE	GRADE	CREDIT HOURS		
			SEM	QTR	CLASS ROOM
TOTAL					

Indicate academic field:

DESCRIPTIVE TITLE	COMPLE-TION DATE	GRADE	CREDIT HOURS		
			SEM	QTR	CLASS ROOM
TOTAL					

Indicate academic field:

DESCRIPTIVE TITLE	COMPLE-TION DATE	GRADE	CREDIT HOURS		
			SEM.	QTR	CLASS ROOM
TOTAL					

Indicate academic field:

DESCRIPTIVE TITLE	COMPLE-TION DATE	GRADE	CREDIT HOURS		
			SEM	QTR	CLASS ROOM
TOTAL					

MISCELLANEOUS COURSES

DESCRIPTIVE TITLE	COMPLE-TION DATE	GRADE	CREDIT HOURS SEM	QTR	CLASS ROOM	DESCRIPTIVE TITLE	COMPLE-TION DATE	GRADE	CREDIT HOURS SEM	QTR	CLASS ROOM
TOTAL						TOTAL					

PART II — PRIVACY ACT STATEMENT AND CERTIFICATION

The Office of Personnel Management is authorized by section 1302 of Chapter 13 (Special Authority) and sections 3301 and 3304 of Chapter 33 (Examination, Certification, and Appointment) of Title 5 of the U.S. Code to collect the information on this form.

Executive Order 9397 (Numbering System for Federal Accounts Relating to Individual Persons) authorizes the collection of your Social Security Number (SSN). Your SSN is used to identify this form with your basic application. It may be used for the same purposes as stated on the application.

The information you provide will be used primarily to determine your qualifications for Federal employment. Other possible uses or disclosures of the information are:

1. To make requests for information about you from any source; (e.g., former employers or schools), that would assist an agency in determining whether to hire you;

2. To refer your application to prospective Federal employers and, with your consent, to others (e.g., State and local governments) for possible employment;

3. To a Federal, State, or local agency for checking on violations of law or other lawful purposes in connection with hiring or retaining you on the job, or issuing you a security clearance;

4. To the courts when the Government is party to a suit; and

5. When lawfully required by Congress, the Office of Management and Budget, or the General Services Administration.

Providing the information requested on this form, including your SSN, is voluntary. However, failure to do so may result in your not receiving an accurate rating, which may hinder your chances for obtaining Federal employment.

ATTENTION — THIS STATEMENT MUST BE SIGNED
Read the following paragraph carefully before signing this Statement

A false answer to any question in this Statement may be grounds for not employing you, or for dismissing you after you begin work, and may be punishable by fine or imprisonment (U.S. Code, Title 18, Sec. 1001). All statements are subject to investigation, including a check of your fingerprints, police records, and former employers. All the information you give will be considered in reviewing your Statement and is subject to investigation.

CERTIFICATION I CERTIFY that all of the statements made in this Statement are true, complete, and correct to the best of my knowledge and belief, and are made in good faith.	Signature (Sign in ink)	Date Signed

COMPLETE PART III ON THE NEXT PAGE IF YOU
CLAIM SUPERIOR ACADEMIC ACHIEVEMENT

PART III - SCHOLASTIC ACHIEVEMENT

NOTE: This part is for the use of college students and graduates who may qualify for some GS-7 positions on the basis of undergraduate scholastic achievement, as provided in an open job announcement. *See the appropriate job announcement for complete requirements.* Proof of scholastic achievement under one of these provisions should not be submitted with your application, but will be required by the hiring agency at the time of appointment. If you do not wish to qualify on this basis or if you do not meet the scholastic requirements for the position, do not complete this part. In any case, YOU MUST SIGN YOUR NAME AFTER THE CERTIFICATION STATEMENT AT THE BOTTOM OF PAGE 3.

A. **COLLEGE OR CLASS STANDING.** Must be in upper third of your graduating class in the college or university, or major subdivision such as School of Engineering, School of Business Administration, etc.

NUMBER IN CLASS _____   YOUR STANDING _____

Proof of class standing should be in the form of a statement in writing from the institution's registrar, the dean of your course of study, or other appropriate official. This statement of class standing must be based on a suitable measure of your academic performance, such as the results of a comprehensive examination or an overall faculty assessment, and must indicate the basis of the judgment. Class standing must be based on your standing in your college or university or the first major subdivision (e.g., the School of Business Administration, the College of Arts and Sciences, etc.). Subdivisions below this level, i.e., a single academic department within a large university, such as the English Department or the Accounting Department, are not recognized as major subdivisions for this purpose.

B. **COLLEGE-GRADE POINT AVERAGE.** Your grade-point average (GPA) should be recorded in the manner that is most beneficial to you, using one of methods below. Your grade-point average must be expressed in terms of a value on a 4.0 scale based on 4 years, the last 2 years, or courses completed in the major field of study.* If computing your GPA, indicate the method used and period covered by checking the appropriate boxes in item 2 *and* in item 3 below, and compute your average in the space provided below on this page.

1. GPA as recorded on final transcript _____ (Transcript must cover *at least* the last 2 years)

2. (Check One)   ☐ Average of undergraduate courses   ☐ Average in major field of study

3. (Check One)   ☐ At time of filing *   ☐ All 4 years   ☐ Last 2 years

* You may be rated provisionally eligible if you are a senior student, provided you have the required average in the junior year. You will be required to submit evidence at the time of appointment that you maintained the required average during your senior year.

In computing your grade-point average, round to the first decimal place, (e.g., 2.95 = 3.0 , 2.94 = 2.9, 3.45 = 3.5, etc.). If your college uses a different system, explain below, or on an attachment, how it compares with the grade-point average on a 4.0 scale:

If more than 10 percent of your courses were graded on a pass/fail or similar system rather than on a traditional grading system, you can usually claim credit under the scholastic achievement provision based only on class standing or membership in a national honor society. The exception is if you can document that only your freshman-year courses (25 percent or less of your total credit) were credited on a pass/fail or similar system.

NO. OF SEMESTER OR QUARTER HOURS AT 4.0 ("A")	_____	X	4 =	_____
NO. OF SEMESTER OR QUARTER HOURS AT 3.0 ("B")	_____	X	3 =	_____
NO. OF SEMESTER OR QUARTER HOURS AT 2.0 ("C")	_____	X	2 =	_____
NO. OF SEMESTER OR QUARTER HOURS AT 1.0 ("D")	_____	X	1 =	_____
NO. OF SEMESTER OR QUARTER HOURS AT 0.0 ("F")	_____	X	0 =	_____
TOTAL (1)	_____	TOTAL (2)		_____

COMPUTED GRADE-POINT AVERAGE   _____
Total (2) divided by Total (1)

C. **HONOR SOCIETY MEMBERSHIP.** Must be one of the national scholastic honor societies meeting the minimum requirements of the Association of College Honor Societies (other than freshman scholarship honor societies).

Name of honor society and date you were elected to membership. _____

GPO 775-752 6 90

SF 15, Application for 10-Point Veteran Preference

The form on the next two pages may be reproduced and submitted with your application if you qualify for a veteran preference. The two-page form lists which people are eligible for the preference, but the following three pages, which come from Chapter 211 of the *Federal Personnel Manual*, **define** the terms in clearer detail. A veteran of the Armed Forces does not necessarily qualify for the ten point preference, while some employees of the Public Health Service and the National Oceanic and Atmospheric Administration (NOAA) **do** qualify! Also, under certain circumstances, the spouse of a living veteran, the widow or widower of a veteran, and the natural mother of some disabled or deceased veterans are eligible for veterans preference points.

Next, there is a page which describes eligibility for Veterans Readjustment Appointment, a special hiring program for some veterans who served during the Vietnam era (5 August, 1964 through 7 May, 1975). The last page in this appendix has a list of points of contact for questions about veterans' preferences.

Note that if you intend to apply for a disabled (or deceased) veteran's ten point preference, you will need to complete an SF 15 **plus** provide official documentation verifying the disability or death. See the SF 15, page two, for further details.

Standard Form 15 (Rev 7/83)
U S Office of Personnel
    Management
FPM Supplement 296-33
FPM Chapter 211

Form Approved
OMB No 3206-0001

APPLICATION FOR 10-POINT VETERAN PREFERENCE
(TO BE USED BY VETERANS & RELATIVES OF VETERANS)

PERSON APPLYING FOR PREFERENCE

1. Name (Last, First, Middle)

2. Name and Announcement Number of Civil Service or Postal Service Exam You Have Applied For or Position Which You Currently Occupy

3. Home Address (Street Number, City, State and ZIP Code)

4. Social Security Number

5. Date Exam was Held or Application Submitted

VETERAN INFORMATION (TO BE PROVIDED BY PERSON APPLYING FOR PREFERENCE)

6. Veteran's Name (Last, First, Middle) Exactly As It Appears on Service Records

7. Veteran's Periods of Service

Branch of Service	From	To	Service Number

8. Veteran's Social Security Number

9. VA Claim Number, If Any

TYPE OF 10-POINT PREFERENCE CLAIMED

INSTRUCTIONS: Check the block which indicates the type of preference you are claiming. Answer all questions associated with that block. The "DOCUMENTATION REQUIRED" column refers you to the back of this form for the documents you must submit to support your application. [PLEASE NOTE: Eligibility for veterans' preference is governed by 5 U.S.C. §2108, 5 CFR Part 211, and FPM chapter 211. **All conditions are not fully described in this form because of space restrictions.** The office to which you apply can provide additional information. Instructions on how to apply for five point preference are on SF 171, Personal Qualifications Statement, or PS Form 2591, Application for Employment (U.S. Postal Service Application).]

DOCUMENTATION REQUIRED
(See reverse of this form.)

☐ 10. VETERAN'S CLAIM FOR PREFERENCE based on non-compensable service-connected disability; award of the Purple Heart; or receipt of disability pension under public laws administered by the VA.

. . . .
A and B

☐ 11. VETERAN'S CLAIM FOR PREFERENCE based on eligibility for or receipt of compensation from the VA or disability retirement from a Service Department for a service-connected disability.

. . . .
A and C

☐ 12. PREFERENCE FOR SPOUSE of a living veteran based on the fact that the veteran, because of a service-connected disability, has been unable to qualify for a Federal or D.C. Government job, or any other position along the lines of his/her usual occupation. (If your answer to item "a" is "NO", you are ineligible for preference and need not submit this form.)

a. Are you presently married to the veteran?
☐ YES ☐ NO

C and H

☐ 13. PREFERENCE FOR WIDOW OR WIDOWER of a veteran.
(If your answer is "NO" to item "a" or "YES" to item "b", you are ineligible for preference and need not submit this form.)

a. Were you married to the veteran when he or she died?
☐ YES ☐ NO

b. Have you remarried? (Do not count marriages that were annulled.)
☐ YES ☐ NO

A, D, E, and G
(Submit G when applicable.)

☐ 14. PREFERENCE FOR (NATURAL) MOTHER of a service-connected permanently and totally disabled, or deceased veteran provided you are or were married to the father of the veteran, *and*
—your husband (either the veteran's father or the husband of a remarriage) is totally and permanently disabled, *or*
—you are now widowed, divorced, or separated from the veteran's father and have not remarried, *or*
—you are widowed or divorced from the veteran's father and have remarried, but are now widowed, divorced, or separated from the husband of your remarriage.
(If your answer is "NO" to item "c" or "d", you are ineligible for preference and need not submit this form.)

a. Are you married?
☐ YES ☐ NO

b. Are you separated? If "YES," do not complete "c." Go to "d."
☐ YES ☐ NO

c. If married now, is your husband totally and permanently disabled?
☐ YES ☐ NO

d. If the veteran is dead, did he/she die in active service?
☐ YES ☐ NO

DISABLED VETERAN:
C, F, and H
(Submit F when applicable.)

DECEASED VETERAN:
A, D, E, and F
(Submit F when applicable.)

PRIVACY ACT STATEMENT

The Veterans' Preference Act of 1944 authorizes the collection of this information. The information will be used, along with any accompanying documentation, to determine whether you are entitled to 10-point veterans' preference. This information may be disclosed to: (1) the Veterans' Administration, or the appropriate branch of the Armed Forces to verify your claim; (2) a court, or a Federal, State, or local agency for checking on law violations or for other related authorized purposes; (3) a Federal, State, or local government agency, if you are participating in a special employment assistance program; or (4) other Federal, State, or local government agencies, congressional offices, and international

organizations for purposes of employment consideration, e.g., if you are on an Office of Personnel Management list of eligibles.

Executive Order 9397 authorizes Federal agencies to use the Social Security Number (SSN) to identify individual records in Federal personnel records systems. Your SSN will be used to ensure accurate retention of records pertaining to you and may also be used to identify you to others from whom information about you is sought. Furnishing your SSN and the other information sought is voluntary. However, failure to provide any part of the information may result in a ruling that you are not eligible for 10-point veterans' preference or in delaying the processing of your application for employment.

I certify that all of the statements made in this claim are true, complete, and correct to the best of my knowledge and belief and are made in good faith. [A false answer to any question may be grounds for not employing you, or for dismissing you after you begin work, and may be punishable by fine or imprisonment (U.S. Code, Title 18, Section 1001).]

This Form Must Be Signed By All Persons Claiming 10-Point Preference

Signature of Person Claiming Preference

Date Signed
(Month, Day, Year)

FOR USE BY APPOINTING OFFICER ONLY
Signature and Title of Appointing Officer

☐ Preference Entitlement Was Verified

Name of Agency

Date Signed
(Month, Day, Year)

PREVIOUS EDITIONS UNUSABLE   15–109   NSN: 7540-00-634-3972

DOCUMENTATION REQUIRED—READ CAREFULLY
(PLEASE SUBMIT PHOTOCOPIES OF DOCUMENTS BECAUSE THEY WILL *NOT* BE RETURNED)

A. DOCUMENTATION OF SERVICE AND SEPARATION UNDER HONORABLE CONDITIONS

Submit any of the documents listed below as documentation, provided they are dated on or after the day of separation from active duty military service.
1. Honorable or general discharge certificate.
2. Certificate of transfer to Navy Fleet Reserve, Marine Corps Fleet Reserve, or Enlisted Reserve Corps.
3. Orders of Transfer to Retired List.
4. Report of Separation from a branch of the Armed Forces.
5. Certificate of Service or release from active duty, provided honorable separation is shown.
6. Official Statement from a branch of the Armed Forces showing that honorable separation took place.
7. Notation by the Veterans' Administration or a branch of the Armed Forces on official statement, described in B or C below, that the veteran was honorably separated from military service.
8. Official statement from the Military Personnel Records Center that official service records show that honorable separation took place.

B. DOCUMENTATION OF SERVICE-CONNECTED DISABILITY (NON-COMPENSABLE, I.E., LESS THAN 10%); PURPLE HEART; AND NONSERVICE-CONNECTED DISABILITY PENSION

Submit one of the following documents:
1. An official statement, *dated within the last 12 months,* from the Veterans' Administration or from a branch of the Armed Forces, certifying to the present existence of the veteran's service-connected disability of less than 10%.
2. An official citation, document, or discharge certificate, issued by a branch of the Armed Forces, showing the award to the veteran of the Purple Heart for wound or injuries received in action.
3. An official statement, *dated within the last 12 months,* from the Veterans' Administration, certifying that the veteran is receiving a nonservice-connected disability pension.

C. DOCUMENTATION OF SERVICE-CONNECTED DISABILITY (COMPENSABLE, I.E., 10% OR MORE)

Submit one of the following documents, if you checked Item 11 on the front of this form:
1. An official statement, *dated within the last 12 months,* from the Veterans' Administration or from a branch of the Armed Forces, certifying to the veteran's present receipt of compensation for service-connected disability or disability retired pay.
2. An official statement, *dated within the last 12 months,* from the Veterans' Administration or from a branch of the Armed Forces, certifying that the veteran has a service-connected disability of 10% or more.

3. An official statement or retirement orders from a branch of the Armed Forces, showing that the retired serviceman was retired because of permanent service-connected disability or was transferred to the permanent disability retirement list. The statement or retirement orders must indicate that the disability is 10% or more.
For spouses and mothers of disabled veterans checking Items 12 or 14, submit the following:
An official statement, *dated within the last 12 months,* from the Veterans' Administration or from a branch of the Armed Forces, certifying: 1) the present existence of the veteran's service-connected disability, 2) the percentage and nature of the service-connected disability or disabilities (including the combined percentage), 3) a notation as to whether or not the veteran is currently rated as "unemployable" due to the service-connected disability, and 4) a notation as to whether or not the service-connected disability is rated as permanent and total.

D. DOCUMENTATION OF VETERAN'S DEATH
1. If on active military duty at time of death, *submit* official notice, from a branch of the Armed Forces, of death occurring under honorable conditions.
2. If death occurred while not on active military duty, *submit* death certificate.

E. DOCUMENTATION OF SERVICE OR DEATH DURING A WAR, IN A CAMPAIGN OR EXPEDITION FOR WHICH A CAMPAIGN BADGE IS AUTHORIZED, OR DURING THE PERIOD OF APRIL 28, 1952, THROUGH JULY 1, 1955

Submit documentation of service or death during a war or during the period April 28, 1952, through July 1, 1955, or during a campaign or expedition for which a campaign badge is authorized.

F. DOCUMENTATION OF DECEASED OR DISABLED VETERAN'S MOTHER'S CLAIM FOR PREFERENCE BECAUSE OF HER HUSBAND'S TOTAL AND PERMANENT DISABILITY

Submit a statement from husband's physician showing the prognosis of his disease and percentage of his disability.

G. DOCUMENTATION OF ANNULMENT OF REMARRIAGE BY WIDOW OR WIDOWER OF VETERAN

Submit either:
1. Certification from the Veterans' Administration that entitlement to pension or compensation was restored due to annulment.
2. A certified copy of the court decree of annulment.

H. DOCUMENTATION OF VETERAN'S INABILITY TO WORK BECAUSE OF A SERVICE-CONNECTED DISABILITY

Answer questions 1–7 below:

1. Is the veteran currently working? ☐ YES ☐ NO If "NO", go to Item 3	2. If currently working, what is the veteran's present occupation?
3. What was the veteran's occupation, if any, before military service?	4. What was the veteran's military occupation at time of separation?

5. Has the veteran been employed, or is he/she now employed, by the Federal civil service or D.C. Government? ☐ YES ☐ NO
If "YES", provide the following:

A. Title and Grade of Position Most Recently, or Currently, Held	B. Name and Address of Agency	C. Dates of Employment From	To

6. Has the veteran resigned from, been disqualified for, or separated from a position in the Federal civil service or D.C. Government along the lines of his/her usual occupation because of service-connected disability? ☐ YES ☐ NO
If "YES", submit documentation of the resignation, disqualification, or separation.

7. Is the veteran receiving a civil service retirement pension? ☐ YES ☐ NO
If "YES", give the Civil Service retirement annuity number _ _ _ _ _ _ _ _ _ _ CSA NUMBER—

Subchapter 2. Entitlement to Preference

2—1. DEFINITIONS

The following definitions are used for the purposes of preference in Federal employment.

(1) "Veteran" means a person who was separated with an honorable discharge or under honorable conditions from active duty in the armed forces performed
- (a) in a war;
- (b) in a campaign or expedition for which a campaign badge has been authorized; *or,*
- (c) during the period beginning April 28, 1952, and ending July 1, 1955; *or,*
- (d) for more than 180 consecutive days, other than for training, any part of which occurred during the period beginning February 1, 1955 and ending October 14, 1976.[1]

Persons who lost their lives under honorable conditions while serving in the armed forces during a period named in (1)(a) through (d) are also referred to as veterans for the purposes of this chapter only. (Refer to FPM Supplement 296-33 for a list of recognized wars, campaigns, and expeditions).

(2) "Active duty," or "active military duty," means full-time duty with military pay and allowances in the armed forces, except for training or for determining physical fitness and except for service in the Reserves or National Guards.

(3) "Armed Forces" means the United States Army, Navy, Air Force, Marine Corps, and Coast Guard.

(4) "Uniformed services" means the armed forces, the commissioned corps of the Public Health Service, and the commissioned corps of the National Oceanic and Atmospheric Administration (formerly the Environmental Science Services Administration, Coast and Geodetic Survey).

---

[1]Section 702 of Public Law 94-502, enacted October 15, 1976 abolishes peacetime preference for those entering active duty after October 14, 1976, *unless* they serve in a campaign or war or meet the definition of "disabled veteran" described in subchapter 2-1(6) of this chapter.

(5) "Discharge under honorable conditions" means either an honorable or a general discharge from the armed forces. The Department of Defense has responsibility for administering and defining military discharges. (An amnesty or clemency discharge does not meet the Veterans' Preference Act requirement for discharge under honorable conditions. Accordingly, no preference may be granted to applicants with such discharges.)

(6) "Disabled veteran"means a person who was separated under honorable conditions from active duty in the armed forces performed at any time and who has established the present existence of a service-connected disability or is receiving compensation, disability retirement benefits, or pension because of a public statute administered by the Veterans Administration or a military department.[2] (Refer to FPM Supplement 296-33 for a list of acceptable evidence.)

(7) "Ex-serviceperson" means a person who was separated from active duty performed in peace or war. (A person on active duty may be an ex-serviceperson because of separation from previous active duty.)

---

[2]If the Veterans Administration recognizes the existence of a service-connected disability arising from an injury or disease incurred while enroute to, at, or returning from, a place of induction or entry into duty, the person is considered to be a disabled veteran. However, even an individual who is receiving compensation, disability retirement benefits, or pension by reason of laws administered by the Veterans Administration is not eligible for preference, unless he or she has met the requirement of having served on active duty, other than for training, as defined in 2-1(2) of this section. Furthermore, the spouse, widow, widower, or mother of such a disabled veteran is not entitled to preference.

An individual who is disabled while undergoing training with a military reserve unit is *not* considered to be a disabled veteran and is not entitled to preference. (1) Five-point. Every veteran as defined in subchapter 2-1(1) of this chapter is entitled to a 5-point preference.[3] However, veterans who are eligible for and take advantage of 10-point preference are not entitled to an additional 5-point preference.

(8) "Spouse" means legal husband or wife. Common law marriages is recognized for preference, if valid under the laws of the place where the parties lived at the time of the marriage.

(9) "Separation" from a spouse means living apart. A separation need not be approved by a court of law but must be bona fide and permanent.

(10) "Legal separation" from a spouse means a separation a *mensa et thoro* (from bed and board) by court decree, which frees the parties but does not dissolve the marriage tie.

2—2. TYPES OF PREFERENCE

There are 7 different types of preference, each with a separate set of requirements. when used for competitive civil service examination purposes, the applicant must first make a passing grade before preference points may be added to the rating score.

(1) Ten-point (disability). Every disabled veteran as defined in subchapter 2-1(6) of this chapter is entitled to 10-point (disability) preference.

(2) Ten-point (compensable disability). A disabled veteran who was separated under honorable conditions from active duty in the armed forces performed at any time and who has a compensable service-connected disability rating of 10 percent or more is entitled to 10-point (compensable disability) preference rather than 10-point (disability) preference.

Because of certain provisions of the Civil Service Reform Act of 1978, employing offices must distinguish between:

(a) those veterans entitled to 10-point preference due to a compensable service-connected disability of less than 30 percent; and

(b) those veterans entitled to 10-point preference due to a compensable service-connected disability of 30 percent or more. (These persons are given additional pass-over and retention rights. They may also be appointed noncompetitively to positions for which they qualified.)

The following types of preference are referred to as derivative preference, because they are derived from the military service of a veteran who is not using the preference:

(3) Ten-point (spouse). The spouse of a disabled veteran is entitled to 10-point (spouse) preference provided that the veteran is disqualified by reason of a service-connected disability for a Federal civil service position along the general lines of his or her usual occupation.

(4) Ten-point (widow or widower). The widow or widower of a veteran is entitled to 10-point (widow or widower) preference under the following conditions:

(a) he or she was not divorced from the veteran;

(b) he or she as not remarried, or the remarriage was annulled; *and,*

(c) the veteran
   — served during a war; *or,*
   — served during the period April 28, 1952 through July 1, 1955; *or,*
   — served in a campaign or expedition for which a campaign badge has been authorized; *or,*
   — died while on active duty that included service specified above provided that the conditions surrounding the death would not have been cause for other than honorable separation.

(5) Ten-point (mother, deceased veteran). The mother of a deceased veteran is entitled to 10-point (mother) preference under the following conditions:

(a) she is the mother of the veteran who died under honorable conditions when on active duty—during a war; *or,*
   — during the period April 28, 1952 through July 1, 1955; *or,*
   — in a campaign or expedition for which a campaign badge is authorized; *and,*

(b) she is, or was, married to the father of the veteran; *and,*

(c) she—lives with her totally and permanently disabled husband (either the veteran's father or her husband through remarriage); *or,*
   — is widowed, divorced, or separated from the veteran;s father but has not remarried; *or,*
   — remarried but is now widowed, divorced, or legally separated from her husband.

(6) Ten-point (mother, disabled veteran). The mother of a living disabled veteran is entitled to 10-point (mother) preference under the following conditions:

(a) She is the mother of the veteran who was

separated under honorable conditions from active duty performed at any time; and

-> (b) the veteran is permanently and totally disabled from a service-connected injury or illness; and <-

(c) she is, or was, married to the father of the veteran; and

(d) she
— lives with her totally and permanently disabled husband (either the veteran's father or husband through remarriage); or,
— is widowed, divorced, or separated from the veteran's father and has not remarried; or,
— did remarry but is now widowed, divorced, or legally separated from her husband.

2—3. DUAL PREFERENCE

Both a mother and a spouse (including widow or widower) may be entitled to preference on the basis of one veteran's service if they both meet the requirements. However, no derivative preference is available if the veteran is living and is qualified for Federal employment.

2—4. PREFERENCE PRESERVED

(1) Service before June 27, 1944. Preference authorized by any law, Executive Order, rule or regulations in effect on June 27, 1944 (the date of the Veterans' Preference Act of 1944) and based on peacetime military service is preserved. However, such peacetime ex-servicepersons (or their spouses or unmarried widows/widowers) have preference only for reduction-in-force purposes. Preserved preference eligibility depends upon the following:

(a) the ex-serviceperson (or spouse or widow/widower) was a Federal employee on June 27, 1944, and has been a Federal employee continuously—since that date without a break in service of more than one workday; or

(b) the ex-serviceperson (or the spouse or widow/widower) was on a register or eligible on June 27, 1944, was appointed from that register, and has been a Federal employee continuously since that appointment without a break in service of more than one workday.

(2) Break in service. For preservation of preference based on peacetime service before June 27,

1944, the time between an employee's separation by reduction-in-force and reemployment from the reemployment priority list is not a break in service.

2—5. MINIMUM SERVICE REQUIREMENT FOR PREFERENCE

a.-> Persons who entered on active duty in the armed forces after October 14, 1976—the closing date for performing peacetime service which qualifies for veterans' preference—do not qualify for preference unless they are disabled veterans under 5 U.S.C. 2108, or serve during a war or in a campaign or expedition for which a campaign badge has been authorized. The statutory minimum length of service requirement described in this section only applies to those ex-servicepersons who may be entitled to preference based on service in a war, campaign, or expedition. It is an additional requirement to be met before an agency or OPM may award preference. A list of campaigns and expeditions appears in FPM supplement 296-33, subchapter 7.

b. Section 408 of Public Law 97-306, enacted October 14, 1982, amended 38 U.S.C. 3103A to clarify the application of the general minimum-service requirement established by Public Law 96-342 enacted September 8, 1980, for Veterans Administration and other veterans' benefits, to the definition of preference eligible under the civil service laws.<-

c. Accordingly, to qualify for veterans' preference in Federal employment, *a person who enlists after September 7, 1980, or* -> *enters on active duty[1]* <- *on or after October 14, 1982, and has not previously completed 24 months of continuous active duty* must:

(1) perform active duty in the armed forces during a war or in a campaign or expedition for which a campaign badge has been authorized, (the long-standing requirement for preference) *and*

(2) serve continuously for 24 months or the full period called or ordered for active duty.

d. Exclusions. The law excepts a person who:
(1) is discharged or released from active duty (a) for a disability incurred or aggravated in line of duty, or (b) under 10 U.S.C. 1171 or 1173 for hardship or other reasons, or
(2) has a service-connected disability which the Veterans Administration determines is compensable.

e. The service requirement does not affect eligibility for veteran's readjustment appointment or for veterans' preference based on peacetime

service exceeding 180 days from 1955 to 1976, or
other qualifying service prior to September 8, 1980.

-> The "enters on active duty" language was added
by statutory amendment to make clear that officers
and others who may begin active duty through
means other than enlistment are subject to the
minimum-service requirement. The original 1980
law only covered persons who enlist. <-

Attachment 1 to FPM Letter 307-15

Veterans Readjustment Appointments
Expanded Job Opportunities in the Federal Service

Public Law 102-16, effective March 23, 1991, makes it even easier for Federal agencies to hire Armed Forces veterans who served during and after the Vietnam era.

The VRA (Veterans Readjustment Appointment) authority is a special hiring program. Eligible veterans do not have to take examinations or compete with nonveteran candidates. VRA appointees are initially hired for a 2-year period. Successful completion of the 2-year VRA appointment leads to a permanent civil service appointment.

⇒ **Who is eligible for a VRA appointment?**
Veterans who served more than 180 days active duty, any part of which occurred during the Vietnam era (August 5, 1964 to May 7, 1975), and have other than a dishonorable discharge, are eligible if they have (1) a service-connected disability or (2) a campaign badge (for example, the Vietnam Service Medal).

Post-Vietnam-era veterans, who entered the service after May 7, 1975 are eligible if they served on active duty for more than 180 days and have other than a dishonorable discharge.

The 180-day service requirement does not apply to veterans discharged from active duty for service-connected disability.

⇒ **How long are veterans eligible for VRA appointments after they leave the service?**
Vietnam-era veterans qualify for a VRA appointment until 10 years after discharge or until December 31, 1993, whichever date is later.

Post-Vietnam-era veterans are eligible for 10 years after the date of their last discharge or until December 17, 1999, whichever date is later.

Eligible veterans with a service-connected disability of 30% or more can be hired without time limit.

⇒ **Are there any other restrictions on eligibility for a VRA appointment?**
No. Under the new VRA law, all veterans described above are eligible. (The law eliminated a previous requirement that VRA appointees have fewer than 16 years of education.)

⇒ **What jobs can be filled under the VRA authority?**
Federal agencies now can use the VRA authority to fill any white collar position up through GS 11, blue collar jobs up through WG 11, and equivalent jobs under other Federal pay systems.

⇒ **How do veterans apply for VRA authority?**
Veterans should contact the agency personnel office where they want to work. Agencies recruit candidates and make VRA appointments directly without getting a list of candidates from OPM. Veterans can get a list of local agency personnel offices from the Veterans Representative at the OPM offices listed on the back of this sheet.

⇒ **Are disabled veterans entitled to special consideration?**
Agencies must give preference to disabled veterans over other veterans.

⇒ **Is training available after appointment?**
In some cases, agencies provide special training programs for VRA appointees. A program could include on-the-job assignments or classroom training.

⇒ **Can VRA appointees work part-time?**
Agencies may be able to set up part-time work schedules for individuals who want to attend school or handle family or other responsibilities.

(over)

United States	Career Entry Group	1900 E Street, NW	CE-100
Office of	Staffing Policy Division	Washington, DC 20415-0001	June 1991
Personnel			
Management			

U.S. Office of Personnel Management
Area Office Veterans Representatives for Employment Inquiries

Alabama
Lee Hockenberry
Huntsville Area Office
(205) 544-5130

Alaska
John Busteed
Anchorage Area Office
(907) 271-3617

Arizona
Jack Mallin
Phoenix Area Office
(602) 640-5809

California
John Andre
Los Angeles Area Office
(818)575-6507

Susan Fong Young
Sacramento Area Office
(916) 551-3275

Mark Gunby
San Francisco Area Office
(415) 744-7216

Colorado
Doris Veden
Denver Area Office
(303) 969-7036

Connecticut
A.J. Dubois
Hartford Area Office
(203) 240-3607

Delaware
(See Philadelphia, PA)

District of Columbia
William Robinson
Washington Area Service
Center
(202) 606-1848

Florida
R.C. McFadyen
Orlando Area Office
(407) 648-6150

Georgia
Ruth Walker
Atlanta Area Office
(404) 221-4588

Hawaii
Charles Tamabayashi
Honolulu Area Office
(808) 541-2790

June 1991

Idaho
(See Washington State)

Illinois
Victoria Jones
Chicago Area Office
(312) 353-8799

Indiana
Sharon Ellet
Indianapolis Area Office
(317) 226-6245

Iowa
(See Kansas City, MO)

Kansas
Veria Davis
Wichita Area Office
(316) 269-6797

Kentucky
(See Ohio)

Louisiana
Melody Silvey
New Orleans Area Office
(504) 589-2768

Maine
(see New Hampshire)

Maryland
Thomas Platt
Baltimore Area Office
(301) 962-3222

Massachusetts
Donald MacGee
Boston Area Office
(617) 565-5926

Michigan
Thomas Bixler
Detroit Area Office
(313) 226-2095

Minnesota
Paul McMahon
Twin Cities Area Office
(612) 725-3633

Mississippi
(See Alabama)

Missouri
Richard Krueger
Kansas City Area Office
(816) 426-5705

Kirk Hawkins
St. Louis Area Office
(314) 539-2341

Montana
(See Colorado)

Nebraska
(See Kansas)

Nevada
(See Sacramento, CA)

New Hampshire
Gloria Dunn
Portsmouth Area Office
(603) 433-0744

New Jersey
Don Hodge
Newark Area Office
(201) 645-2376

New Mexico
Rosa Benavidez
Albuquerque Area Office
(505) 766-1099

New York
Walter Chasin
New York Area Office
(212) 264-0442

Larry Burkett
Syracuse Area Office
(315) 423-5650

North Carolina
Ayn Clayborne
Raleigh Area Office
(919) 790-2817

North Dakota
(See Minnesota)

Ohio
John McConnell
Dayton Area Office
(513) 225-2529

Oklahoma
Dan Henderson
Oklahoma City Area
Office
(405) 231-4613

Oregon
(See Washington State)

Pennsylvania
John Glooch
Harrisburg Field Office
(717) 782-4546

Gene Hyden
Philadelphia Area Office
(215) 597-7670

Pennsylvania (continued)
George Horn
Pittsburgh Area Office
(412) 644-4355

Puerto Rico
Viven Fernandez
San Juan Area Office
(809) 765-5620

Rhode Island
(See Connecticut)

South Carolina
(See North Carolina)

South Dakota
(See Minnesota)

Tennessee
Ralph Bunten
Memphis Area Office
(901) 544-3958

Texas
Frank McLemore
Dallas Area Office
(214) 767-9133

Jose Borrero
San Antonio Area Office
(512) 229-6613

Utah
(See Colorado)

Vermont
(See new Hampshire)

Virgin Islands
(See Puerto Rico)

Virginia
Valerie DeMeis
Norfolk Area Office
(804) 441-3362

Washington (State)
Robert Coleman
Seattle Area Office
(206) 553-4691

West Virginia
(See Ohio)

Wisconsin
(See Illinois)

Wyoming
(See Colorado)

APPLICATION PACKAGE LOG SHEET

Job Series, Grade and Title: _____

Target Agency: _____ **Closing Date:** _____

Point of Contact: _____ **Phone #:** _____

Date Package Was Sent: _____

Follow-up Action   Date   Remarks

INDEX

G
General Attorney, 10
General Inspection,
    Investigation and
    Compliance Officer, 10-11
General Investigator, 11
General Schedule, 27-28
General Schedule
    Occupations, 101-119
Goals, 8

I
Immigration Inspector, 11
Inspectors General, 12
Investigator, 48

J
Job:
    announcements, 37-38,
    120-131
    series, 9
    vacancies, 4
Jobs:
    entry level, 2-3
    federal, 1
    general schedule, 27-28

L
Law enforcement careers, 1

M
Military experience, 25
Myths, 18-25

O
Office of Personnel
    Management, 40-42

P
Park Ranger, 9, 13
Plans, 8
Police Officers, 10

Positions, 9-12
Pay (see Salaries)
Position management, 29-33
Position Qualification
    Standards, 132-146
Positions, 101-119

Q
Qualifications, 50-53

R
Register, 39-40
Resources, 68-72

S
Salaries, 27-28, 86-88
Security Guard, 10
Security Specialist, 9
Special hiring programs, 53-54
State employment offices, 44

T
Ten Point Veteran
    Preference, 54
Tests, 4
Terminology, 75-83

U
United States Marshal, 10

V
Vacancy announcements, 2-3, 37

W
Work experience, 16-17, 30

X
X-118 Qualification Standards
    Handbook, 75-83

CAREER
RESOURCES

Contact Impact Publications to receive a free annotated listing of career resources or visit their Web site for a complete listing of career resources:
http://www.impactpublications.com.

The following career resources, many of which are mentioned in previous chapters, are available directly from Impact Publications. Complete the following form or list the titles, include postage (see formula at the end), enclose payment, and send your order to:

IMPACT PUBLICATIONS
9104-N Manassas Drive
Manassas Park, VA 22111-5211
Tel. 703/361-7300 or Fax 703/335-9486
E-mail address: impactp@impactpublications.com

Orders from individuals must be prepaid by check, moneyorder, Visa or MasterCard number. We accept telephone, fax, and e-mail orders.

Qty.	TITLES	Price	TOTAL
	GOVERNMENT AND PUBLIC SERVICE JOBS		
__	Applying For Federal Jobs	$17.95	_____
__	Book of U.S. Government Jobs	$18.95	_____
__	Book of U.S. Postal Exams	$17.95	_____
__	Civil Service Handbook	$9.95	_____

189

__ Complete Guide to Public Employment $19.95   _____
__ Complete Guide to U.S. Civil Service Jobs $9.95   _____
__ Directory of Federal Jobs and Employers $21.95   _____
__ Federal Applications That Get Results $23.95   _____
__ Federal Jobs in Law Enforcement (Smith) $14.95   _____
__ Federal Resume Guidebook $34.95   _____
__ Find a Federal Job Fast! $13.95   _____
__ Government Job Finder $16.95   _____
__ How to Get a Federal Job $15.00   _____
__ The KSA Sampler $12.95   _____
__ Reinvented Federal Job Application Forms Kit $6.95   _____
__ Using Today's Reinvented Vacancy Announcement $12.95   _____

NONPROFITS

__ Finding a Job in the Nonprofit Sector $95.00   _____
__ Jobs and Careers With Nonprofit Organizations $15.95   _____
__ Non-Profit's Job Finder $16.95   _____

MILITARY TO CIVILIAN TRANSITION

__ Beyond the Uniform $12.95   _____
__ From Air Force Blue to Corporate Gray $17.95   _____
__ From Army Green to Corporate Gray $17.95   _____
__ From Navy Blue to Corporate Gray $17.95   _____
__ Job Search: Marketing Your Military Experience $16.95   _____
__ Retiring From the Military $24.95   _____

JOB SEARCH STRATEGIES AND TACTICS

__ Change Your Job, Change Your Life $17.95   _____
__ Complete Job Finder's Guide to the '90s $13.95   _____
__ Dynamite Tele-Search $12.95   _____
__ Electronic Job Search Revolution $12.95   _____
__ Five Secrets to Finding a Job $12.95   _____
__ How to Get Interviews From Classified Job Ads $14.95   _____
__ How to Succeed Without a Career Path $13.95   _____

INTERNATIONAL, OVERSEAS, AND TRAVEL JOBS

__ Almanac of International Jobs and Careers $19.95   _____
__ Complete Guide to International Jobs & Careers $13.95   _____
__ Guide to Careers in World Affairs $14.95   _____
__ Jobs for People Who Love Travel $15.95   _____
__ Jobs in Russia and the Newly Independent States $15.95   _____
__ Jobs Worldwide $17.95   _____

RESUMES, LETTERS, & NETWORKING

__ 200 Letters for Job Hunters $19.95   _____
__ Best Resumes for $70,000+ Executive Jobs $14.95   _____
__ Dynamite Cover Letters $13.95   _____

__ Dynamite Networking for Dynamite Jobs	$15.95	_____
__ Dynamite Resumes	$13.95	_____
__ Electronic Resume Revolution	$12.95	_____
__ Electronic Resumes for the New Job Market	$11.95	_____
__ Great Connections	$19.95	_____
__ High Impact Resumes and Letters	$14.95	_____
__ How to Work a Room	$9.95	_____
__ Job Search Letters That Get Results	$15.95	_____
__ The Resume Catalog	$15.95	_____
__ Resumes for Re-Entry: A Woman's Handbook	$10.95	_____

INTERVIEWS & SALARY NEGOTIATIONS

__ 60 Seconds and You're Hired!	$9.95	_____
__ 101 Dynamite Questions to Ask at Your Job Interview	$14.95	_____
__ Dynamite Answers to Interview Questions	$11.95	_____
__ Dynamite Salary Negotiation	$12.95	_____
__ Interview for Success	$15.95	_____
__ Sweaty Palms	$8.95	_____

SUBTOTAL _____

Virginia residents add 4½% sales tax _____

POSTAGE/HANDLING ($5.00 for first
title and $1.50 for each additional book) $5.00
Number of additional titles x $1.50 ----------- _____

TOTAL ENCLOSED ---------------- _____

SHIP TO:

NAME _____

ADDRESS _____

_____

_____

❏ I enclose check/moneyorder for $ _____ made
   payable to IMPACT PUBLICATIONS.

❏ Please charge $ _____ to my credit card:

Card # _____

   ❏ Visa   ❏ MasterCard   ❏ American Express

Expiration date: _____/_____

Signature _____